ID0787420

The
# GNOSTICS

# The
# GNOSTICS

*Myth, Ritual, and Diversity
in Early Christianity*

David Brakke

*Harvard University Press*

*Cambridge, Massachusetts*

*London, England*

*2010*

*Library of Congress Cataloging-in-Publication Data*

Brakke, David
The Gnostics : myth, ritual, and diversity in early
Christianity / David Brakke.
p.   cm.
Includes bibliographical references (p.   ) and index.
ISBN 978-0-674-04684-9
1. Gnosticism.   2. Church history—Primitive and early church,
ca. 30–600.   I. Title.
BT1390.B69 2010
273'.1—dc22      2010018570

*To Bentley Layton*

# CONTENTS

# PREFACE

This book argues for a particular approach to the study of ancient "Gnosticism" and its rejection by "the Church." As the traditional story goes, a multiform religious movement, Gnosticism, arose in the first two centuries CE either as a mutation of Christianity or Judaism or as an independent religion that rapidly became intertwined with Christianity. Gnosticism—whether Sethian Gnosticism or Valentinianism or, later, Manichaeism—posed a serious threat to the Church, which was influenced by but eventually rejected it. The rejection of Gnosticism proved to be as crucial to the Church's developing orthodox character as its balanced acceptance and rejection of elements of "paganism" and Judaism.

In recent years both of the key characters in this story, Gnosticism and the Church, have received heightened scrutiny from historians. As for "Gnosticism," some scholars argue that there was no single religious phenomenon that we can identify as Gnosticism in antiquity, and so the category itself is seriously flawed and should be discarded. Others continue to think that Gnosticism either provides an important and useful way to categorize a variety of religious movements or names an actual religion that did exist. As for "the Church," most scholars agree that there was no single Church in the first and second centuries, but a multitude of competing groups, one of which began to emerge in the third century as the dominant one and so can be called "proto-orthodoxy." Others argue that even this picture of competing groups, because it creates rigid boundaries and static identities for discrete Christian groups and schools, fails to capture the full diversity of Christian traditions before Constantine.

In this book I argue for a middle position on both of these questions. I agree that the category "Gnosticism," as traditionally conceived, does not serve a useful purpose and does not accurately identify an actual ancient religion. But I claim that there was in fact a Gnostic school of thought, the literary remnants of which can be identified and therefore can be described and studied, albeit sketchily. In turn, I agree that the model of competition between a proto-orthodoxy and other Christian groups has flaws and can underestimate diversity. But I believe, too, that Christian groups did engage in practices of self-differentiation that constructed boundaries between rival Christians and that certain streams of Christian tradition (e.g., the Gnostics) can be identified. The catholic orthodoxy that emperors and bishops sought to establish in the fourth and later centuries did not appear out of nowhere but found a path laid for it in the self-defining activities of pre-Constantinian Christians.

I freely admit that most of what I argue here is not original to me. Indeed, my approach to the Gnostics draws explicitly on those of Mark Edwards, Alastair Logan, and especially Bentley Layton, although I differ with each of these scholars on some details. It identifies the tradition that scholars often call "Sethian Gnostics" as the Gnostic school of thought and argues that the thought and practice of only these Christians should be considered "Gnosticism" (if indeed one should even use this term). This middle way on the question of Gnosticism has not found as much support among historians of early Christianity as other approaches, perhaps because it does not completely reject the evidence of heresiologists like Irenaeus but engages it critically, or because it is often confused with a typological approach. In any event, I shall argue for its superiority over both the traditional concept of a wide-ranging "Gnosticism" and the refusal to speak of ancient Gnostics or a Gnostic myth at all.

In the first chapter I describe and assess recent approaches to Gnosticism and Christian diversity in the first three centuries CE. I then turn to the categories "Gnosticism" and "the Church." In Chapter 2 I explain how we can identify the Gnostics of antiquity and their literature, and in Chapter 3 I provide a description of the basic teachings and rituals of this early Christian movement. These chapters seek to circumscribe the scope of the term "Gnostic" as the label for a religious movement and to reveal its fundamentally Christian character. In Chapters 4 and 5, I discuss how various early Christian groups and individuals sought to differentiate themselves from Christians with whom they disagreed and so to create a "true" Christianity. Chapter 4 focuses on three key figures in second-century Rome (Valentinus, Marcion, and Justin Martyr), and

Chapter 5 examines the strategies of self-differentiation that select Christians of the second and third centuries employed.

Nearly all the Gnostic writings that I discuss can be found in Bentley Layton, *The Gnostic Scriptures: A New Translation with Annotations and Introductions* (Garden City, N.Y.: Doubleday, 1987), the overall plan of which represents the perspective of this book; others are available in Marvin Meyer, *The Nag Hammadi Scriptures: The International Edition* (New York: HarperOne, 2007). I have used the translations in Layton's *Gnostic Scriptures*, but have regularly altered them to conform to my translations of names and technical terms. Additional important ancient sources are listed in the bibliography. Using these works, readers can explore for themselves the thoughts of the Gnostics, Valentinians, and other early Christians.

This book originated when I was invited to write a chapter entitled "Self-Differentiation among Christian Groups: The Gnostics and Their Opponents" for the first volume of the *Cambridge History of Christianity* (Cambridge: Cambridge University Press, 2006), 245–260. I am grateful to the editors, Margaret Mitchell and Frances Young, for their invitation and for their learned responses to my early drafts. My colleague and friend Stephen Emmel also read an early draft of that essay, and he encouraged me to expand what I had written into a book and thus set me on this path.

In the years that followed, I presented my ideas to audiences at Harvard Divinity School, Ohio State University, and the annual meeting of the Society of Biblical Literature. Ismo Dunderberg, Antti Marjanen, and the other members of the Gnosticism seminar at the University of Helsinki read and discussed drafts of the first two chapters, and I am very grateful for their perceptive questions and suggestions and for Ismo's generous written comments on the entire book. Bert Harrill read multiple drafts with his usual insight and eye for errors and ambiguities.

At Harvard University Press, Margaretta Fulton helped me formulate the original plan of the book, and later Sharmila Sen supported my work with patience, sage advice, and good humor. The excellent anonymous readers for the Press offered numerous corrections and suggestions for improvement.

Meanwhile, my colleagues in the Department of Religious Studies at Indiana University cheerfully endured a chair who did not carry out his administrative duties with undivided attention.

More than anything I have written so far, however, this book owes both its existence and its content to my students, both undergraduate and graduate. For over fifteen years, in my courses "Gnostic Religion and Literature" and "Christianity, 50–450," they have asked questions and offered insights that have shaped every page. As I wrote, I envisioned readers like them—bright, curious, but not (yet) experts in Gnostic esoterica. I can hardly name them all here, but I want to single out Ken Fisher for his enduring skepticism about everything I say here, Austin Busch and Ellen Muehlberger for their willingness to interpret Gnostic works just as they would any other early Christian literature, and Laura DeLancey and Phil Dorroll for their comments on parts of this book in draft.

I first read Gnostic and Valentinian works closely in Coptic with Bentley Layton, the key elements of whose approach to "Gnosticism" I have adopted. Although he will not agree with everything in this book and cannot be held responsible for how I present even his own ideas, to him should be attributed the spirit of considering the Gnostics from the wider perspective of early church history, not as exotic "others," but as part of the social and intellectual diversity that makes early Christianity so fascinating.

# ABBREVIATIONS

AH          Irenaeus, *Against the Heresies* (*Detection and Overthrow of Gnōsis Falsely So-Called*)

*Ap. Adam*   *The Revelation of Adam (The Apocalypse of Adam)*

*Ap. John*   *The Secret Book According to John (The Apocryphon of John)*

*FP*         Origen, *On First Principles*

*Gos. Eg.*   *The Holy Book of the Great Invisible Spirit (Egyptian Gospel)*

*Hyp. Arch.* *The Reality of the Rulers (The Hypostasis of the Archons)*

*Mar.*       *Marsanes*

*Str.*       Clement of Alexandria, *Stromateis*

*Zōs.*       *Zōstrianos*

The

# GNOSTICS

# 1

## IMAGINING "GNOSTICISM" AND EARLY CHRISTIANITIES

In the spring of 2006, a group of scholars captured headlines across the globe by publishing a new early Christian work, *The Gospel of Judas*. Although it was originally composed in Greek, it survives now only in a Coptic translation found in a fragmentary manuscript probably from the fourth century CE. Some of the text is now lost, but what remains surprised and fascinated millions of people. According to this gospel, the original disciples of Jesus and their followers were deluded worshippers of a false god; their primary ritual, the Eucharist, far from a solemn commemoration of the sacrifice of Christ, in fact was leading Christians to their own spiritual deaths. Only Judas knew the true nature of the divine, the real mission of Jesus, and the origin and fate of this world— for Jesus revealed these matters to him alone. As the original publishers of the gospel interpreted it, Judas was not a wicked traitor, but the only disciple who truly understood Jesus and who advanced his mission by facilitating his arrest and crucifixion. Even if scholars would later question this positive view of Judas's character in the *Gospel of Judas*, the contents of this work appeared remarkably different from expected Christian teachings. As one prominent scholar put it, the *Gospel of Judas* represents "Christianity turned on its head."[1]

The earliest Christian author to mention the *Gospel of Judas* agreed with this assessment. He was Irenaeus, the bishop of Lyons in Gaul (France), who wrote his famous *Detection and Overthrow of Gnōsis Falsely So-Called* (or *Against the Heresies*) around the year 180. Irenaeus had read or at least heard about the *Gospel of Judas*, and he called it the fabrication of a group of false Christians, the Gnostics. The Gnostics and others like them, Irenaeus said, composed "miserable fables" that were foreign to true doctrine. In Irenaeus's view there was only one authentic way of being Christian, and so an alternative view of Christian faith must be false, not really Christianity at all. In fact, he argued that Jesus had taught the single authentic Christian doctrine to his disciples, who then transmitted it to their successors, bishops like Irenaeus, who led communities of true Christians throughout the world. People and groups who followed other forms of Christian teaching had deviated from this one true Christianity in diabolically diverse ways.

And yet, Irenaeus said, all these false versions of Christianity, however different they were, stemmed from a single demonic teacher, Simon Magus. Simon appears in the Acts of the Apostles as a magician who offered the apostles money for the power to bestow the Holy Spirit (Acts 8:9–24). Moreover, Irenaeus argued that all these teachers and groups manifested false *gnōsis* or knowledge, which St. Paul had warned against in one of his letters to Timothy (1 Timothy 6:20). The *Gospel of Judas*, then, indeed turned Christianity on its head, for it was not Christianity at all, rather yet another demonically inspired example of false *gnōsis*.

As a bishop, Irenaeus saw it as his job to enforce proper Christian belief, and in fact many elements of Irenaeus's version of Christianity eventually became key features of later Christian orthodoxy. When modern scholars say that a work like the *Gospel of Judas* turns Christianity on its head, they are probably not trying to enforce proper Christian belief as Bishop Irenaeus was, but they are working with a way of understanding the development of early Christianity that it is similar to Irenaeus's. That is, they know what "Christianity" is, and they know that the *Gospel of Judas* subverts that. On the one hand, there is a lot of truth to this way of seeing things. The vast majority of Christians, both in antiquity and today, do not share the views of the *Gospel of Judas*. The Christianity that came to dominate the Roman world and to shape the present-day varieties of the faith looked a lot more like Irenaeus's religion than that of *Judas*. On the other hand, *that* Christianity—the Christianity of Irenaeus—was not *the* Christianity when the *Gospel of Judas* first appeared. The Christians who produced and read *Judas* were doubtless sincere in their beliefs and considered themselves the true Christians. They did not know that they were turning Christianity on its head; they thought they were teaching true Christianity, and they severely criticized other Christians as hopelessly deceived. The failure to include *Judas* in the eventual canon of the New Testament was neither historically inevitable nor (the historian would say) the result of divine intervention.

Rather, it was the result of a complex process in which differing forms of Christianity competed with, influenced, borrowed from, and rejected each other.

One of the challenges facing those of us who study ancient Christianity—or who study any religion in any period—is how to understand both the coherence and the diversity of a religious tradition. With early Christianity this challenge is particularly acute because eventually Christianity did establish an orthodoxy, albeit never completely and not without challenge, and thus it seems natural now to think of something like the *Gospel of Judas* as not true Christianity. How can we imagine early Christianity in a way that does justice to both of these factors—great diversity and yet an eventual orthodoxy?

In this effort, the legacy of Irenaeus has continued to affect how historians think in at least two important ways. First, his view that Christianity started out as a single, fairly uniform religion and then became more diverse, whether for good or for ill, has remained influential. Scholars may not share Irenaeus's confidence that Jesus himself taught a true Christian doctrine that later bishops faithfully preserved, but they have at times reproduced his basic story in their own ways. For example, the great nineteenth-century German theologian Adolf von Harnack argued that the essence of Christianity is to be found in the original preaching of Christ, but this essential Gospel developed into orthodox dogma through a process of adaptation to Greek culture (or "Hellenization") that was both necessary and tragic. On the one hand, Christian teaching needed to become more sophisticated and explain itself in philosophical terms acceptable to learned Greek speakers. On the other hand, various Christian groups went off course and became "heretics" when they adopted too many Greek ideas, like the Gnostics, or when they stuck too closely to their Jewish roots, like the so-called Ebionites. Or, trying to move beyond Harnack and yet to explain why Christianity changed in the first few centuries, we historians of today depict the early Christians as needing to establish their identity by differentiating themselves from Greco-Roman paganism on the one hand and from Judaism on the other—and sometimes there is a third alternative, Gnosticism. Diversity resulted as Christians responded to these challenges in different ways. That there is a single thing called "Christianity," however diverse, is not really questioned. Irenaeus would not be happy with even this rather benign notion of development, but he would be familiar with the concept of a single original Christian message that later diversified (wrongly, to his mind) as it carried its message into the pluralistic culture of the Roman Empire.

Irenaeus continues to shape how historians think in a second way. He argued that the various "heretical" Christian groups that he condemned, such as the Gnostics and the Valentinians and the Marcionites, were all manifestations of a single erroneous phenomenon, false *gnōsis*, or, as we call it today, "Gnosticism." It is noteworthy that Irenaeus's true and false versions of Christianity to some extent mirror one another. Both originated in a single person, whether Jesus or Simon Magus, and both were handed down through a chain of successive leaders, whether orthodox bishops or heretical teachers. But there is a crucial difference: the bishops who transmitted Christian truth did not alter it in any way, although they may have further developed certain teachings in defense of the faith and under the guidance of the Holy Spirit. But the heretical teachers who transmitted the false *gnōsis* of Simon constantly changed and elaborated on their teachings. So it is not Christianity that is diverse, but false *gnōsis*. Irenaeus and his fellow orthodox Christians are all the same, while the heretics differ widely in their teachings and go by all sorts of names: Gnostics, Sethians, Valentinians, Marcionites, Carpocratians, and so on. But this heretical diversity is somewhat illusory; in actual fact, all these heresies are a manifestation of false *gnōsis*.

When modern scholars depict many different ancient groups as belonging to the same category—Gnosticism—they replicate Irenaeus's notion of false *gnōsis* but neglect his careful delineation of its diversity. Indeed, historians today sometimes go beyond even what Irenaeus claimed and assert that Gnosticism was an independent religion of its own that existed before Christianity and later included Manichaeism and Mandaeism, religions that did not appear until the third and perhaps fifth centuries, respectively. Just as Irenaeus believed that, despite their surface diversity, all the heresies shared similar features of false *gnōsis*, so, too, modern scholars make lists of the features that characterize all the diverse movements that they say represent Gnosticism. And just as Irenaeus believed that all the heresies had a single origin in Simon Magus, scholars try to discern precisely when and where Gnosticism originated, with Greek-speaking Judaism now the most popular hypothesis. To be fair, the motives of these scholars are benign: they want to see Gnosticism not as a Christian heresy, as Irenaeus did, but as a substantive religion or worldview in its own right. Still, their basic approach to ancient beliefs about Jesus that did not turn out to be orthodox reflects that of Irenaeus.

Contemporary scholars face the challenge of moving beyond the picture of early Christianity and "Gnosticism" that Irenaeus presents, even while we must still depend on him for much crucial information about the Christianity of his day. In the rest of this chapter I address both problematic facets of Irenaeus's vision—a single, original orthodoxy and a single, multifaceted Gnosticism. In each case I argue for an approach that neither replicates that of Irenaeus nor matches completely that of his severest modern critics. In my view, we must endeavor as fully as possible to recognize the difference between the categories and typologies that modern scholars create in order to make sense of disparate yet related phenomena, on the one hand, and the communities and traditions that ancient Christians sought to create (not always successfully) to worship God and share their teachings, on the other. The problem is, of course, that even when we are delineating and describing ancient groups, we are also imagining and elaborating our own categories.

## The "Varieties" of Early Christianity and Their Limits

As we imagine how Christianity (or Christianities) developed in the first three centuries, we need to account for two things. On the one hand, Christians were strikingly diverse and disagreed about nearly everything. Although some Christian leaders sought to control this diversity and create unity and uniformity, they were not able to do so. On the other hand, when in the early fourth century Constantine became the first Roman emperor who not only tolerated but also actively supported Christianity, the idea that Christians should form a single, worldwide "orthodox" Church took hold quickly. The diverse Christian groups of the earliest period often attempted to create unified organizations that spanned the Mediterranean. In the fourth and subsequent centuries, bishops and emperors made great progress in establishing a single Church, although they never did so with complete success. Any model for Christian diversity in the pre-Constantinian era must recognize not only the persistence of diversity but also the rise of orthodoxy, not only the hybridity and fluidity of early Christian writings and movements but also the unity and bounded character of many of them.

Irenaeus's model of a single true Christianity from which heretics diverged readily accounts for both of these factors. According to this view, there always was a single true orthodox faith, and any Christian "diversity" simply reflects demonically inspired heretical movements. Modern versions of this model allow that "mainstream" Christianity may have changed and developed over the centuries, but they still insist that a core set of Christian beliefs persisted within this mainstream and that groups like the Montanists and the Valentinians strayed from these basic beliefs in various ways. One feature that both Irenaeus and his modern successors share is the idea of the priority of orthodoxy and the subsequent nature of heresy, both chronologically and intellectually. The North African theologian Tertullian was the first to clearly articulate this idea, which claims that "heretics" always reject or distort orthodox, mainstream, or widely shared Christian ideas and practices.[2] And so orthodoxy precedes heresy, both in time—orthodoxy came first, with the original apostles—and in logic—heretical teachings distort or oppose orthodox ones. Or, in its less orthodox modern version, most Christians shared a set of core beliefs, which other groups either dissented from or took to unfortunate extremes.

Walter Bauer took a major step in dismantling the Irenaean model of early Christianity when he published his landmark 1934 book, *Orthodoxy and Heresy in Earliest Christianity*.[3] Examining earliest Christianity in selected regions, Bauer argued that in some locations, such as Egypt and Mesopotamia, forms of Christianity that would later be deemed heretical actually predated what would later emerge as orthodox. Orthodoxy did not in fact always precede heresy. Bauer argued that in the first few centuries, a wide variety of early Christian groups competed with each other for converts and argued about their beliefs. No overall power structure existed that could enforce one single point of view. The idea of a single orthodoxy arose in the city of Rome, whose cultural elite often liked conformity and dominance, and then spread to other regions. Real enforcement of orthodoxy across the Mediterranean came in the fourth century, when Constantine converted to Christianity and put the power of the imperial state behind it.

Subsequent studies have called into question nearly all of Bauer's specific historical reconstructions. For example, while Bauer thought that the earliest Christians in Egypt were Gnostics, evidence now suggests that they were Jews from Palestine who did not hold beliefs that anyone would call Gnostic.[4] Still, Bauer's central insights—that Christianity was diverse from the get-go, that it developed in different ways in different regions, and that the emergence of orthodoxy was the result of real struggle—are now accepted as the basis for understanding Christianity in the early centuries. These ideas form the fundamental principles of a new model of early Christian development, the "varieties of early Christianity" model. In this view, there never was a single Christianity; rather, a variety of Christian groups competed with one another in the early years. One form of Christianity eventually came to dominate in several regions of the ancient Mediterranean world, but only after a period of struggle. Although it became the basis for what later Christians would understand to be orthodox Christianity, before the fourth century its eventual triumph was not ensured, and so it is best to call it "proto-orthodoxy" during the period before Constantine.

To explore this model's virtues and shortcomings, we can use an analogy that Church historian Philip Rousseau briefly offers as a way to understand how scholars approach the diversity of early Christian Egypt. When we construct narratives of how proto-orthodoxy competed with and overcame its rival Christian groups, the result, Rousseau writes, is "like watching the rerun of a race while fixing your eyes confidently on the outsider you know to have won as he inches unexpectedly forward along the fence."[5] Rousseau goes on to offer his own helpful critique of this way of thinking. Following his lead, we can think of the varieties-of-early-Christianity model as something like a horse race. In this model, we cannot really see the starting gate, but around the year 100 CE, numerous independent Christian communities come into view, none with a fully convincing claim to exclusive authenticity as "true Christianity." They jostle for position and argue with one another about which of them are the true Christians. In hindsight we can identify the "horse" that will emerge as the dominant orthodoxy by the end of the third century: it is represented by Irenaeus and other early Christians such as Justin Martyr, Clement of Alexandria, Origen, Hippolytus of Rome, Tertullian (before he "became a Montanist"), and others. We call this form of Christianity "proto-orthodoxy," because there is not yet an orthodoxy, but it will grow into it. We watch proto-orthodoxy as it competes with and overcomes its rivals, setting itself up as the horse that Constantine will ride, so to speak.

Another metaphor for this way of viewing early Christianity is warfare, which appears in the title of Bart Ehrman's recent book, *Lost Christianities: The Battles for Scripture and the Faiths We Never Knew.*[6] Here the Gnostics, the Marcionites, and others are "lost Christianities" in two senses. First, they have become lost to later Christians because most of their writings were destroyed and their teachings forgotten; thanks to recent discoveries of some of their texts, however, contemporary scholars can recover them. The most important of these discoveries was a set of Coptic books found near Nag Hammadi in Egypt in 1945; the Nag Hammadi works represented an astonishing variety of "lost Christianities," including "Gnostic" ones. Second, these alternate forms of Christianity (*not* "heresies") were literal losers: they lost the battle for Christianity to proto-orthodoxy. The proto-orthodox Christians won their victory with an "arsenal" of "weapons," including apostolic succession, the rule of faith, the biblical canon, and the like. Here the metaphor is a battle, not a horse race, but the basic idea remains competition and struggle among diverse early Christian groups, with proto-orthodoxy emerging as the winner.

Whether we think of it as a horse race or as a battle, the varieties-of-early-Christianity model marks a real improvement over the Irenaean paradigm and its modern successors. It recognizes diversity and tries not to privilege the proto-orthodox horse, which is just one of several competitors in the race. It does not have any single origin for either orthodoxy or heresy. There are many horses in the race when it starts, and some join the race later. It not only admits that early Christians seriously disagreed about fundamental aspects of the faith; it highlights these disagreements as the central factor that shaped the form of Christianity that later emerged as orthodoxy. For all these reasons, this model is a very useful one that we must not discard completely.

But scholars increasingly see the flaws in this approach and are trying to construct a more dynamic picture. We can start with the metaphor of competition itself: even if the model does not privilege the proto-orthodox horse, that horse does win the race. And, as with all competitions, this result invites analysis: Why did this variety of Christianity win out? It must not be due solely to Constantine's choice of it. Surely, scholars muse, there must have been features of proto-orthodoxy that enabled it to prevail over its rivals or even guaranteed its success, and surely the Gnostics and Valentinians and Marcionites must have had flaws that prevented them from winning—elitism, lack of moral clarity, or whatever. Karen King has described how even historical projects that have endeavored to give the Gnostics their say and not to view them through the lens of their enemies turn out to have been efforts to discover the normative center of legitimate Christian identity.[7] That is, scholars have asked: How can we differentiate the Gnostics from those we now know are the winning Christians and so see what made proto-orthodox Christianity successful and—dare we say it?—more legitimate and even true? The winning side is usually the "better" side.

Normative theological reflection on the development of Christianity is not necessarily a bad thing, but when we seek to define one stream of Christian tradition and discover its legitimating essence, not only what made it what it was but also what other forms of Christianity ought to have been, then we inevitably distort its competitors as they fail to measure up or as they contain some good features at the cost of others. For example, we may note that the Montanists differed from the proto-orthodox by allowing women to hold leadership positions in their churches—good thing!—but to do so they relied on a highly charismatic and therefore poorly organized mode of church structure—bad thing!

Another problematic feature of the horse-race model is that horses are—thank goodness—discrete bounded entities, clearly distinct from one another. Racing horses do not really change through their competition with each other. We might say that a horse develops its abilities or the jockey adjusts his strategies through interaction with their competitors, but we often think of this as sharpening or improving an already set identity. So, too, the predominant way of imagining the varieties of Christianity depicts them as discrete bounded groups: here is Pauline Christianity, there is Johannine Christianity, and then come the Gnostics, the Valentinians, the Montanists, the Marcionites, the Encratites, Jewish Christianity, the proto-orthodox, and so on. In the laudable effort to emphasize the diversity of early Christian groups and movements, we tend to create stable "name brands," which interact and compete with each other like so many brands of breakfast cereal on a grocery store shelf. The characteristics that we have assigned to each group determine its success or failure. Proto-orthodoxy itself, the real object of our interest, may clarify or sharpen its characteristics or beliefs through competition with its rivals, but it does not change in any fundamental way. The proto-orthodox always knew, for example, that the God of the Hebrew Bible and the Father of Jesus Christ were the same God, but it was pressure from the Gnostics, the Valentinians, and the Marcionites that helped the proto-orthodox to clarify and articulate that belief. Or, to shift the metaphor, Marcion may have been the first Christian to establish a clear canon of Scriptures, and the proto-orthodox may have done so in response to him and to other groups, but the idea of a Bible with both Old and New Testaments was a natural development of the proto-orthodox commitment to both the Jewish Scriptures and the Gospel, helped along by interaction with other groups.

Increasingly, however, scholars are less inclined to see religious groups as so distinct and well defined. The boundaries between groups are not clear: people and ideas travel back and forth and all around socially and intellectually. As Robert Campany has put it, religions are neither "fully integrated systems" nor "containers into which persons, ideas, practices, and texts may be fit without remainder."[8] Religious people do not settle neatly into our groups, and groups in antiquity (which did exist, of course) created their identities through interaction with others in a dynamic process. We will need to return to this point.

Finally, any conception of "the varieties of early Christianity" that places a single proto-orthodoxy within a plurality of "other groups" re- tains one key aspect of the Irenaean view: that proto-orthodoxy was single and consistent wherever it was found, while other forms of Chris- tianity were multiple and diverse. But, as we shall see, in several impor- tant ways such proto-orthodox teachers as Justin Martyr and Clement of Alexandria had more in common with, say, Valentinus than they did with Bishop Irenaeus. There was no single and uniform proto-orthodoxy, but multiple modes of piety, authority, and theology that later ortho- doxy represents as its forerunners. The Church and critical scholarship depict as "proto-orthodox" people and groups who might well have initiated trajectories that would not have culminated in Nicene ortho- doxy and who might be surprised to find themselves depicted as "the same." Clement and Irenaeus may have agreed that the Gnostics were wrong about the character of the God of Genesis, but Clement was skeptical of bishops and claimed that Christ taught a secret *gnōsis* to his apostles, who then passed it down to learned teachers like himself. Val- entinus would have agreed with this idea, while Irenaeus would not. But even Irenaeus himself was more similar to the Gnostics he hated than he would care to admit. He condemned the Gnostics for creating an elabo- rate series of divinities and heavenly realms and for tracing salvation genealogically through the sons of Adam. But Irenaeus himself described a series of seven heavens ruled by various powers, and he, too, traced the blessings of God genealogically through the sons of Noah.[9] So there was no single proto-orthodox horse in the race, nor was there a single proto- orthodox army in the war: proto-orthodoxy itself was highly diverse and, in many respects, not very orthodox.

So we have now seen two basic and influential models for imagining the diversity of early Christianity and the emergence of orthodoxy: the Irenaean model of a single Christianity that develops and diversifies, and the horse-race model of a number of Christianities that compete with one another until a winner emerges. The second model is far preferable to the first, but it, too, has shortcomings that fail to do justice to the complexity of the ancient situation. Is a new model emerging that will guide how we think about early Christianity? I think not if we seek a model as clear and straightforward as the two that we have examined, but several scholars advocate an approach that focuses on "identity formation." Karen King describes this approach in this way:

> It aims to understand the discursive strategies and processes by which early Christians developed notions of themselves as distinct from others within the Mediterranean world (and were recognized as such by others), including the multiple ways in which Christians produced various constructions of what it means to be Christian. Methodologically, it is oriented toward the critical analysis of practices, such as producing texts; constructing shared history through memory, selective appropriation, negotiation, and invention of tradition; developing ritual performances such as baptism and meals; writing and selectively privileging certain theological forms (e.g., creeds) and canons; forming bodies and gender; making place and marking time; assigning nomenclature and establishing categories; defining "others" and so on.[10]

This fruitful perspective shifts our focus away from discrete groups, the "varieties" of early Christianity, to the strategies by which individuals and groups sought to define themselves. The historian does not take for granted the existence of defined groups, but instead interrogates how ancient people sought to create, transform, and challenge religious communities and practices. "We should," Robert Campany argues, "think of the coherence of such imagined communities as something repeatedly claimed, constructed, portrayed, or posited in texts, rituals, and other artifacts and activities, rather than as simply given."[11]

Three key themes characterize this new work on early Christian diversity: hybridity, rhetoric, and ethnicity. All of these themes reflect the growing influence of cultural studies, especially postcolonial perspectives, in the fields of early Christianity in particular and of religious studies in general. By investigating how new cultural forms are created and continually revised in an imperial context, postcolonial studies in particular has much to offer the study of early Christianity in the Roman Empire. Let me say a bit about the utility of the concepts of hybridity, rhetoric, and ethnicity, and why I think that, despite all that I have said, we need still to retain something from our earlier ways of approaching early Christian diversity.

First, hybridity. Within religious studies the term "hybridity" functions something like the old "syncretism." It marks the mixing, combining, and grafting of disparate cultural elements. But, while syncretism tended to work as the opposite of purity and so seemed to have a negative value, hybridity highlights cultural inequality within an empire and the ways that dominant and subordinate cultures mutually interact and create new cultural forms that are never pure or completely distinct. Hybridity suggests a process that is both inevitable and creative, indeed the only process by which subcultures flourish and grow.[12] For those of us in religious studies, the notion of hybridity complicates our reliance on such highly productive theoretical concepts as "worldview" or "system of symbols." In its most popular version, the result of reading such theorists as Peter Berger and Clifford Geertz, "worldview" and related concepts have helped us to see how religious symbols and social practices combine to form integrated subcultures in which people find meaning.[13] But this perspective has also led us to see stability, harmony, and holism where there is usually contestation, conflict, and continual reinterpretation of cultural materials.[14] Within early Christian studies, an emphasis on hybridity as the norm challenges traditional characterizations of Gnostics and other early Christians as particularly syncretistic and highlights the creative combination of cultural elements in proto-orthodox figures such as Irenaeus. The boundedness, continuity, and natural evolution of incipient beliefs and doctrines that we have attributed to early Christian groups were not in fact there in social life, but were invoked rhetorically in the multilateral process of identity formation and boundary setting in which all early Christians were engaged.

Rebecca Lyman, for example, draws on the notion of hybridity to approach one of proto-orthodoxy's star architects, Justin Martyr.[15] She places Justin's invention of the idea of heresy (which I shall discuss in Chapter 4) in the context of a wider discussion of universalism and multiple traditions occurring in the second century, a time when numerous Greek-speaking authors, like Justin, were attempting to find a place for varieties of Hellenism within Roman imperial domination. Justin's idea of heresy does not reflect an already formed and essentially intolerant

Christian proto-orthodoxy, but rather represents one of a range of attempts by Hellenistic thinkers (mostly not Christian) to relate notions of universal truth and local beliefs. Lyman contests a picture of Christianity as inherently less tolerant and prone to impose an orthodoxy than other ancient religious movements, although she admits that Christians are often "more extreme" than others. And, indeed, I would observe that we do not find too many other ancient religions with bishops. But Lyman's important move is to dislodge our notion of some essential orthodoxy that Justin defends or even creates and to situate Christian discussions of plurality and universal truth within a wider cultural setting. Justin fully participates in dominant Hellenistic and Roman cultures even as he contests them—the condition of hybridity.

The role of rhetoric is the second feature of recent attention to early Christian diversity. If Christians like Justin were not easily differentiated from other ancient religious people and in fact shared even in the cultures that they claimed to reject, then they faced the challenge of asserting such a difference in their rhetoric. "It may be that some imagined 'others' are strictly necessary for the claiming of an 'own' identity and coherence."[16] Here the most important scholar is the French theologian Alain Le Boulluec. His 1985 book on the idea of heresy in Greek literature of the first three centuries argued that, for all his virtues, Walter Bauer had still seen "orthodoxy" and "heresy" as actual things, whether those things are ideas or social groups.[17] Bauer may have highlighted struggle and diversity, but he knew orthodoxy and heresy when he saw them. Instead, Le Boulluec studied "heresy" as a representation, constructed diversely by various authors, and thus as a product of discourse, as was indeed "orthodoxy." It functioned as a way to imagine "others" against whom one can claim one's legitimate identity. Recent scholars often claim that Le Boulluec himself did not go far enough, but they are all indebted to his claim that "orthodoxy"/"heresy" was a discourse designed to construct boundaries and create identity. Thus, scholars increasingly follow Le Boulluec's example by studying how authors such as Irenaeus, Hippolytus, and Tertullian created different notions of heresy in their projects of intellectual and social formation.

Finally, the language of ethnicity and citizenship played an important role in the rhetorics of self-differentiation. Here early Christian studies participate in a renewed discussion of ethnicity, especially Greekness, that is taking place in classical studies and ancient history. Christians called themselves a "third race" (in addition to "Jews" and "Gentiles" or

"Greeks" and "barbarians"), and among them the Gnostics identified themselves as "the seed of Seth" or "the immovable race." Thus, Denise Buell explores in her recent book how various Christian authors used ethnic or racial language to establish identity and to construct boundaries between themselves, non-Christians, and other Christians. In each case Buell treats Christian identity not as something given, but as something constructed, challenged, and legitimated. To claim "orthodoxy" emerges as one strategy in such identity formation.[18] Similarly Benjamin Dunning examines how Christians used the language of foreignness and civic belonging to express and shape their identities.[19] As much as these studies contribute to a wider conversation about ethnicity in antiquity, they represent also a belated recognition among scholars of early Christianity of the inextricable connection between religion and ethnic identity in ancient culture.[20] The recognition of the fundamental tie between the gods and ethnicity or genealogy can shed better light on such Gnostic self-identifications as "the seed of Seth."

All of these themes—hybridity, rhetoric, and ethnicity—make problematic the reigning paradigm of "varieties of Christianity" or, as I have called it, the horse-race model, because they emphasize the difficulty of delineating clear boundaries between the brands of Christianity that we see as in competition. They tend to dissolve the distinctions that both ancient Christians and modern scholars have made among early Christian groups and movements not only by dissolving boundaries but also by highlighting diversity among sources that we have grouped together as representing "Gnosticism" or "proto-orthodoxy." If such distinctions are mainly rhetorical categories that served to create difference more than they simply reflected it, then such groups lose their place in what we would call the real world of ancient society, and scholars are encouraged to engage primarily in microstudies, examinations of how individual texts or authors draw on a wide range of cultural resources to create their diverse visions of "Christianity." We should instead explore each "novel way cultural elements are now put to work, by means of such complex and ad hoc relational processes as resistance, appropriation, subversion, and compromise."[21] A good example of this is Karen King's recent book on *The Secret Book According to John,* which examines this text not as a representative of "Gnosticism," but on its own as the creative combination of different traditions into a new Christian story.[22]

Advocates of these new approaches often criticize any attempts to make larger claims about differing modes of religious authority or to delineate and describe particular forms of or groups within Christianity. They maintain that we must not "reify" either our categories or those of the ancients, but we should maintain a constant appreciation for the fluidity of boundaries and the hybridity of identities. In a moment, I shall examine how scholars in the study of "Gnosticism" have taken a bundle of characteristics, unevenly distributed across a variety of ancient sources, and created a religious entity that had no actual existence in the ancient world.

Scholarly anxiety about reification of categories and the rigidity of boundaries is justified, but I argue it need not cripple efforts to describe real social and religious distinctions among ancient Christians. For example, perspectives that emphasize rhetoric and discourse too often neglect the importance of social practice. Heresy was indeed an invention, but not one created through rhetoric alone. Rather, it was created also through practices such as excommunication, ritualized condemnation, and silencing of texts. Cohesion of religious groups was not just a function of shared ideas; it was also the effect of such practices as repeated rituals, exchange of letters and gifts, and patronage. For example, Irenaeus did not just write books that labeled others as heretics; he and his fellow bishops could fire priests who had "heretical" views, suppress certain theological writings, and exchange gifts only with other bishops with similar doctrines. Such practices had real social effects. Boundaries among early Christian groups may have been porous and in constant need of reassertion, but sometimes they did exist. Our goal should be to see neither how a single Christianity expressed itself in diverse ways, nor how one group of Christians emerged as the winner in a struggle, but how multiple Christian identities and communities were continually created and transformed.

Certainly historians of early Christianity must absorb as fully as we can the rhetorical, representational, and hybrid character of our sources, but if we are to appreciate truly the diversity of early Christianity and not dissolve that diversity into a soup of hybridity, we still need to make distinctions among forms of Christian life. And if we are to account for the rapid and aggressive emergence of the totalizing discourse of Nicene Christianity in the fourth century, we must recognize not only that pre-Nicene Christians were trying to construct boundaries that were not there, but also that sometimes they managed to do so successfully. We cannot and should not return to Irenaeus's vision of a clear orthodoxy marching to an inevitable triumph over heresy, but neither can we ignore a seemingly persistent feature of Christianity: its drive to create in social reality the single "body of Christ"—a body composed of many and diverse members, to be sure—but one body nonetheless.

In this effort, it is important to distinguish between at least two kinds of categories in the study of ancient Christianity. On the one hand, modern scholars sometimes develop interpretive categories in order to analyze and label modes of religious thought and practice for a variety of purposes. For example, we speak of "apocalyptic Judaism" or "apocalyptic eschatology" in order to group together and highlight religious works, people, and movements that differed in many ways but shared certain broad characteristics. Calling the thought of both, say, Paul and the Qumran community "apocalyptic Judaism" need not suggest either that Paul and the Jews of Qumran belonged to the same Jewish group or that they shared all the same views and practices, but it does legitimately identify them as sharing a similar approach to issues of revelatory knowledge about God's plans, the restoration of Israel, the interpretation of Scripture, the injustice of the current world order, and the like. In this respect they differed from a Jew such as Philo of Alexandria, who interpreted Jewish traditions through more philosophical categories and did not show much interest in an imminent end-time.

The category "apocalyptic Judaism" is heuristic or interpretive: it functions as a tool for comparison and allows us to signal certain aspects of Paul's thought without having to explain them in full. It helps us to place Paul within a recognizable stream of Jewish theology. Paul and the Jews of Qumran would not describe themselves as belonging to this category, and they might even deny that they share elements of the same worldview at all, but that is not the point: the category helps modern people to understand. It is hard to imagine being able to carry out the work of history without such interpretive categories as "apocalyptic Judaism" or "Platonism."

On the other hand, scholars develop social categories that they believe correspond, usually imperfectly, to how ancient people actually saw and organized themselves. For example, scholars of early Christianity routinely speak of "Johannine Christianity," by which they mean a tradition associated with the Gospel of John and the three Letters of John in the New Testament. These four works share a distinctive vocabulary and pattern of thought that set them apart from other texts in the New Testament and from early Christianity generally, and they seem to reflect the peculiar history and experience of a specific group of Christians. Scholars argue about the particular characteristics of this hypothetical group (for example, where to locate it geographically), and certainly no member of the group would have identified herself as a "Johannine Christian." But many, if not most, scholars believe that the hypothesis of such a group best accounts for the surviving literary evidence, and it enables us to describe more precisely how the Christianity of even the earliest period was not a single movement, but a collection of diverse groups with distinctive beliefs and practices. Obviously the detection and description of such groups, traditions, and movements among early Christians function as essential tools of the "varieties of early Christianity" (or horse-race) model.

Although we can distinguish these two kinds of categories, in actual practice nearly all the categories that scholars of religion use are a hybrid of these kinds. Or, better, even our social categories are also interpretive ones. Consider, for example, "Christianity." On the one hand, it is surely a social category that reflects accurately how numerous people throughout history have identified themselves and organized their religious communities. When, however, we include the apostle Paul and his followers in "Christianity," the category becomes more interpretive or heuristic. To be sure, Paul worshipped Jesus Christ, and his writings now make up a significant part of the Christian Bible. But Paul did not use the term "Christian" for himself or "Christianity" for what he taught—these words had not yet been invented, as far as we can tell.[23] He understood himself to be a Jew, preaching the fulfillment of the Jewish tradition. Paul, then, belongs firmly to the history of Judaism, and it is somewhat misleading to use the terms "Christian" and "Christianity" in discussing him. And yet we do use such terms—and rightly so, for Paul and his churches belong just as firmly to the history of Christianity as well, even if they did not see themselves in this way. It would distort understanding of Christianity to deny this. We see, then, that even a category that appears "simply" to reflect social reality, that identifies a tradition that truly existed and saw itself so, in fact functions also interpretively, including data that scholars assign to it apart from the self-understanding of religious people. Scholars are inventing and shaping whatever categories they use.

Work on early Christian history falls into confusion when scholars fail to distinguish our two kinds of categories, both of which (we must always remember) we ourselves have created, or even more so, when we fail to attend to how our necessarily hybrid categories are functioning. Certainly interpretive categories like "apocalyptic Judaism" can be misapplied or poorly conceived, can obscure rather than enhance understanding, and so forth—and in such cases they need to be discarded or reformed. And certainly social categories like "Johannine Christianity" can be misapplied or poorly conceived, can obscure rather than enhance understanding, and so forth—and in such cases they need to be discarded or reformed. Scholars are engaged in this kind of activity all the time, and it does not call into question the utility of having such categories, just the utility of the ones under critique and reform.[24]

The confusion of category types or inattention to how categories function can indeed lead scholars to question the use of any kind of categories. Karen King, for example, has effectively and persuasively demonstrated that the category "Jewish Christianity" has little heuristic value because it means different things to different scholars. Sometimes it functions purely interpretively to include different groups that share similar features (as does "apocalyptic"), and sometimes it functions socially to circumscribe certain groups (as does "Johannine Christianity"). The term has been applied to Christian groups that have too little in common and differ too much in their relationship to Judaism to be included in the same category. It does not truly map onto any Christian group for which we have reliable (rather than merely polemical) evidence. A major problem that her analysis uncovers is that many scholars appear not to have considered whether "Jewish Christianity" functioned as an interpretive category (like "apocalyptic") or a social one (like "Johannine Christianity"), or they slip between these two functions without seeing that they are doing so.[25] It does not follow from King's excellent critique, however, that, because this confused category does not work, scholars should not still try to discern how early Christians themselves coalesced into social groups. That is, the failure of a particular interpretive or social category, no matter how spectacular, need not call into question the utility and viability of such categories. To be sure, we need to avoid "a fixed and essentialized categorization of early Christian multiformity,"[26] but we need not abandon the quest to discern the actual groups, traditions, and movements that made up the jumble of "ancient Christianity." And, in fact, I believe that this lesson is the one that we can apply to scholarly constructions of "Gnosticism" as well.

## "Gnosticism" and Its Limits

"Gnosticism" is an outstanding example of a scholarly category that, thanks to confusion about what it is supposed to do, has lost its utility and must be either abandoned or reformed. "Gnosticism," as we have seen, is a legacy of Irenaeus, who characterized all of the Christian groups that he opposed as examples of false *gnōsis* and as originating in Simon Magus. Still, even Irenaeus recognized that the several groups that he described were in fact not the same group and disagreed strongly with one another. Indeed, he emphasized this point as an indication that such groups therefore could not have the single truth of Christian faith. His descriptions, as polemical and distorted as they are, make real distinctions between various teachers and schools and their doctrines. Irenaeus provides unwitting testimony to the great variety of the Christianity of his day.

The story of how modern scholarship has developed the idea of Gnosticism has been told several times, and its details need not detain us here.[27] Suffice it to say that in the seventeenth century Henry More (1614–1687) invented the term "Gnosticism" for all the heresies that Irenaeus and his heresiological successors attacked. In the centuries that followed, scholars developed, refined, and debated theories of how Gnosticism arose and interacted with Christianity. During this period historians included in "Gnosticism" a variety of movements that were dualistic, that is, ones that sharply differentiated spiritual reality from material existence and the soul from the body, valuing the soul and the spiritual and deprecating the body and the material. Such groups also distinguished between the god who created this material world and the ultimate God: a lower, inferior god created this universe, not the utterly transcendent spiritual God, who is too remote to have done so. Dualism and a lower creator god have remained key, even defining, features of Gnosticism for most scholars. Before the late nineteenth century, historians had only the accounts of authors like Irenaeus to work with, and so they were eager to embrace potential new sources for Gnostic beliefs when they began to appear around the turn of the twentieth century. Some "new sources," like the literature of the Mandaeans, led scholars down ultimately unproductive paths, but not so the many newly discovered Coptic manuscripts, especially those found at Nag Hammadi in 1945. These Coptic texts included works that undeniably came from or were related to the "Gnostics" that Irenaeus described, although exact correspondences were very few.

Two examples of "Gnosticism" from the late twentieth century exemplify the result of this process of combining long-known heresiological reports with an abundance of new evidence. First, a 1966 conference in Messina took as one of its goals the construction of a definition of Gnosticism that a wide range of scholars could accept. The participants decided that "Gnosis" should be taken to refer to the general idea of knowledge reserved for an elite group and thus is a widespread phenomenon in the history of religions. True Gnosticism, however, was to be found in the seemingly Christian systems of the second century, and they defined it by "a coherent series of characteristics," primarily the ideas of (1) "a divine spark" in humanity that came from the spiritual realm and to which people must be awakened and (2) "a downward movement of the divine" (often called Wisdom) into the realm of fate to recover lost divine energy. Gnosticism features "a dualistic conception on a monistic background, expressed in a double movement of devolution and integration." Gnosticism's notion of divine "devolution" means that it cannot belong to "the same historical and religious type as Judaism or the Christianity of the New Testament and the Grosskirche [i.e., 'the Great Church' or 'proto-orthodoxy']." From this the participants constructed a Gnosticism that was neither Judaism nor Christianity, but could be linked with the *Upanishads* of ancient India and the Cathars of medieval Europe.[28]

The second example is Kurt Rudolph's important book *Gnosis,* which appeared in German in 1977 and in English translation in 1983. It rapidly became the book that graduate students in ancient Christianity had to read to get up to speed on Gnosticism. Rudolph's Gnosticism was "a dualistic religion, consisting of several schools and movements," which took "a negative attitude toward the world and the society of the time" and "proclaimed a deliverance" from "the constraints of earthly existence through 'insight.'"[29] Making full use of the Nag Hammadi documents, Rudolph told a story of breathtaking scope and diversity: Gnosticism was an independent religion, which originated in Simon Magus (as Irenaeus had said) and then diversified to include Basilides, Valentinus, Marcion, *The Gospel According to Thomas,* and other texts and persons, eventually blossoming into Manichaeism, Mandaeism, and the Bogomils of medieval Europe. Here, indeed, it seems that an interpretive category based on certain characteristics (dualism, negativity about the world and society, deliverance, "insight") had somehow, with or without the scholar's cognizance, morphed into a social category, an actual religion that survived for centuries. This Gnosticism is a religion in which probably few adherents would recognize the others as in fact belonging to the same religion as they do. Its different schools and movements could teach strikingly different ideas, tell myths with completely different casts of characters, and consider different books to be scriptures—and yet they are all "Gnosticism."

As Gnosticism became a religion seemingly without boundaries, the people and texts that scholars assigned to it assumed the characteristics of that religion, even if they did not display them. That is, scholars knew—from this or that "Gnostic" text, or from this or that report from a Church Father—that Gnostics were dualists, that they believed in a lower creator god, that they hated the world and society, that they did not believe that Christ was truly human, and that their disdain for the body led them either to adopt extreme asceticism or to live as wanton libertines. No matter if a text from Nag Hammadi did not contain such ideas or even seemed to contradict them; that text still belonged to Gnosticism and must somehow reflect its characteristics.

Understandably, the bloated and distorting nature of "Gnosticism" has led some scholars to argue that the entire category should simply be abandoned. Michael Williams's 1996 book *Rethinking "Gnosticism"* presents a devastating critique of the category "Gnosticism."[30] By comparing the mythologies and teachings of four persons or documents that scholars usually have called "Gnostic"—*The Secret Book According to John,* Ptolemy the Valentinian, Justin's *Baruch* (not Justin Martyr), and Marcion of Sinope—Williams exposes the distortion that is required to imagine that they all belonged to any movement more restricted than "Christianity." "Gnosticism," Williams persuasively argues, has become meaningless by saying both too much and too little. It includes under its umbrella people and texts that are far too many and far too diverse, and therefore it provides no real understanding of them. He goes on to deconstruct many of the clichés that have come to be associated with "Gnostics"—for example, that their interpretations of the Bible constitute a dramatic "reversal" of biblical narrative, that they are religious "parasites" who attach their anticosmic worldview to already existing traditions, and that they are either sexually licentious or strictly ascetic. Instead, Williams shows that the surviving works that scholars have assigned to "Gnosticism" both display considerable variety and take positions that are not outrageously radical within their historical contexts.

Williams grants that some of the people and texts of traditional "Gnosticism" share some features and concerns that make it fruitful for them sometimes to be studied together. He proposes a new interpretive category, "biblical demiurgical traditions," which would include "all those that ascribe the creation and management of the cosmos to some lower entity or entities, distinct from the highest God," as they "also incorporate or adapt traditions from Jewish or Christian Scripture."[31] Such a category would function more like "apocalyptic": it highlights certain shared characteristics and provides a convenient grouping for study, but does not imply that all the included traditions share all the same features or form a distinct religion or movement. As welcome as this turn to an explicitly interpretive rather than social category is, "biblical demiurgical traditions" has its own problem: namely, it is hard to imagine a Jew or Christian of the first few centuries CE who would not belong to it. As we shall see, all Jews and Christians with any philosophical interests ascribed the creation of this world (in full or in part) to a deity lower than the highest God and also interpreted and adapted Jewish or Christian Scriptures. As the Gospel of John put it, God did not create the world directly; rather, "all things came into being" through God's Word (John 1:3). Thus, even "biblical demiurgical traditions" may be too large a category (larger even than "Gnosticism"?) to be truly useful. More helpful is Williams's complementary proposal to delineate smaller and more distinct sociohistorical traditions, such as Valentinianism, from the people and texts that used to belong to "Gnosticism."

Karen King offers a more ethically and theologically oriented critique of "Gnosticism." If Williams argues that the category distorts our knowledge of early Christian persons and groups, King claims that scholars have followed Irenaeus and the other ancient heresiologists by using it to define normative Christianity and to render certain forms of Christianity illegitimate. The modern category "Gnosticism," she argues, "reinscribes and reproduces the ancient discourse of orthodoxy and heresy."[32] In so doing, modern historians create a false picture of Christian groups in the second and third centuries, which in fact lacked a defined orthodoxy. They tend to reify and essentialize the polemical categories of ancient persons like Irenaeus and the scholarly categories that they themselves create. In my terms, they turn interpretive categories into social ones, whether unwittingly or not. But even more importantly, the category "Gnosticism" tends to undermine liberating theological reflection in the present by reaffirming so-called "orthodoxy" and branding alternative Christian possibilities as "Gnostic." Instead, historians should seek "not to destroy tradition but to open up space for alternative or marginalized voices to be heard within it. A fuller historical portrait of religious piety can enrich the funds of religious tradition, providing more complex theological resources to attend to the complex issues of our own day." In this way "faith" can be "strengthened and enriched."[33]

Unlike Williams, King does not offer an alternative interpretive category; moreover, she appears to resist most attempts to delineate actual movements, schools, or subcultures within the umbrella of Christianity. In line with the recent trends of thought concerning early Christianity that I discussed above, she fears that such attempts create groups that are too tidy and thus fail to capture the hybrid and fluid situation among early Christianities. She criticizes the "essentializing" of persons and groups into social things that have stable and fixed characters. Instead, she advocates careful attention to and sustained self-awareness of our use of any categories, and she believes in the close reading of individual texts for their distinctive attempts to articulate visions of Christian salvation.[34]

Williams and King are the most prominent advocates of a complete dismantling of "Gnosticism" and the eschewing of the term "Gnostic." In response to their views, defenders of "Gnosticism" have made a range of counterproposals. These suggestions differ in the extent to which they imagine Gnosticism to be an actual religion, but they do rely on a typological approach in which a set of characteristics gathers together similar people and texts. For example, several scholars suggest that a category "Gnosticism" or "Gnosis" that includes several different and even socially and historically unrelated groups can be useful for scholarly purposes. Christoph Markschies argues that "typological constructs . . . help to see phenomena with related content." As the basis for a model of "Gnosis," he proposes a set of eight characteristics, which includes the distinction between a lower creator god and an "other-worldly, distant, supreme God"; an experience of alienation from the world; the notion of a divine spark within the human being; and a tendency toward dualism. On the one hand, Markschies argues that some of the ancient movements that are gathered together by his model were closely connected and that "some of their influence extends to the present." On the other hand, he cautions that the connections among the movements may range from "direct historical" ones to a "common cultural climate" to simple "agreement in content."[35] For him, then, Gnosis is not a single religion. Rather, the teachings of some early "forerunners" of Gnosis, such as Valentinus, paved the way for true systems of Gnosis, such as Valentinianism and "Sethianism," which culminated in Manichaeism, in which Gnosis does indeed take the form of its own religion.

Other scholars propose less elaborate typologies. Antti Marjanen reduces the defining characteristics of Gnosticism to two ideas: that there is or are "(an) evil or ignorant world creator(s) separate from the highest divinity" and that "the human soul or spirit originates from a transcendental world and, having become aware of that, has the potential of returning there after life in this world." Like Markschies, Marjanen does not claim that his Gnosticism was a single religion in antiquity: it is "a heuristic scholarly construct" or "a typologically defined category . . . by which one can group ancient religious texts and thinkers for closer analysis and comparison."[36] At the center of Marjanen's Gnosticism lie Valentinian and "Sethian" works, with a variety of texts, especially from Nag Hammadi, that cannot be classified beyond being "Gnostic."

Marvin Meyer offers a definition of "Gnostic religion" that is also simpler than Markschies's but goes in a different direction from that of Marjanen. "Gnostic religion," he argues, "is a religious tradition that emphasizes the primary place of gnosis, or mystical knowledge, understood through aspects of wisdom, often personified wisdom, presented in creation stories, particularly stories based on the Genesis accounts, and interpreted by means of a variety of religious and philosophical traditions, including Platonism, in order to proclaim a radically enlightened way and life of knowledge."[37] Meyer's definition lacks both of Marjanen's two elements (evil or ignorant creator god and the soul's transcendent origin and goal) and instead emphasizes mysticism, wisdom, and creation stories. Meyer concedes that not all Gnostic texts will fully conform to his definition, and it is not clear how committed he is to imaging a single "religious tradition" as a continuous social entity. For him, "Gnostic religion" appears to mean "a Gnostic type of religion or spirituality," not a single religious tradition that developed over decades or centuries like Christianity or Judaism. His difference with Marjanen can be seen in how each treats *The Gospel According to Thomas*. For Meyer, it has "Gnostic tendencies" because of its emphasis on mystical knowledge, but for Marjanen, it is simply not Gnostic because it lacks an evil or ignorant creator god.[38]

As different as their individual proposals are, Markschies, Marjanen, and Meyer all seek to retain a typologically constructed "Gnosticism" (or "Gnostic religion" in Meyer's case) that scholars understand to be an interpretive or heuristically useful category, not a single ancient religion. In contrast, Birger Pearson argues vigorously that Gnosticism was a religion in its own right.[39] He notes that Ninian Smart had argued that a religion has seven dimensions: doctrinal/philosophical, mythic/narrative, practical/ritual, experiential/emotional, ethical/legal, social/institutional, and material. Pearson examines the Coptic texts from Nag Hammadi, especially *The Secret Book According to John*, and finds that, collectively, they provide evidence for all seven of these dimensions, and thus the Gnosticism that they represent qualifies as a religion. The seven dimensions provide the framework for Pearson's typological construction of Gnosticism: for example, under the doctrinal/philosophical dimension, he includes the split between the supreme God and the lower creator god. Pearson includes even the Mandaeans in his Gnostic religion. Gnosticism, in his view, was a religion distinct from Christianity, although, to be sure, it appears at times to Christianize. Certain Nag Hammadi texts suggest that Gnosticism originated apart from Christianity, and the Mandaeans represent a persistent branch of non-Christian Gnosticism. The Valentinians may have claimed to be Christians, but the "central core" of their message was an "emphasis on gnosis as the basis for salvation"—hence, they, too, belong to Gnosticism (222).

Of these recent typologically oriented proposals, Pearson's is the easiest to criticize because it so faithfully reproduces all the problems of previous scholarship. To be sure, when he argues that Gnosticism is its own religion, distinct from Christianity, he seeks to avoid the reductionism and denigration that attends viewing it as simply an aberration from "orthodox" or "mainstream" Christianity. Pearson wishes to give Gnostic religion the respect that it deserves. Still, his case is not persuasive. By showing that Nag Hammadi and Mandaean texts evince all seven of Smart's dimensions of a religion, Pearson has shown only that these materials can be analyzed as being religious, that is, as coming from a religion or religions, not that they therefore constitute a single independent religion. As the Valentinian case makes clear, Pearson relies heavily on an emphasis on *gnōsis* as the means of salvation to distinguish Christian-looking Gnosticism from Christianity proper, which emphasizes faith (and Jewish-looking Gnosticism from Judaism proper, which emphasizes observance of Torah) (202). But surely an emphasis like this cannot serve to define one religion in distinction from another; rather, it represents a choice among various ways of explaining salvation that might be found within a large number of religious traditions, including Christianity.

Finally, Pearson's argument that the "exotic" Mandaeans represent a continuation of Gnosticism must elide very significant differences between the Mandaean myth and those of the Sethians and the Valentinians (223). Mandaean authors may have drawn on earlier Gnostic and Valentinian writings in their mythmaking, but so, too, did they draw from other traditions, such as Islam. If we return to Smart's seven dimensions of a religion, Valentinian and Mandaean sources may both exhibit practical/ritual dimensions, but they do not share the same rituals; they may both evince social/institutional dimensions, but no one has demonstrated continuity between their social institutions. But Pearson's bar for establishing that two sources come from the same religion is, in the case of Gnosticism, quite low. He considers Manichaeism "a special instance of the larger religious phenomenon called Gnosticism or the Gnostic religion," but the only link between Mani and earlier Gnostics that he adduces is that "the prophet, highly educated as he was, had access to Gnostic literature of a Sethian stamp" (282). In other words, Mani read earlier Gnostic texts and used them. But Mani read and used a variety of religious texts, including the New Testament.

The typological proposals of Markschies and the others avoid Pearson's problem of positing an independent religion without convincing continuity in mythology, ritual, or social institutions, but these proposals are nonetheless unsatisfactory as well. Consider Marjanen's attractively simple reduction of a typology to only two elements: (an) evil or ignorant creator god(s), and the soul's transcendent origin and ultimate goal. It may indeed be intellectually fruitful to study together the people and texts that this definition collects, but why call them "Gnosticism"? For one thing, it is not clear how the term "Gnosticism" follows from the two elements named, neither of which has a necessary connection to *gnōsis*. As we shall see, even ancient heresiologists did not call all of the people and myths that they opposed "Gnostics," and ancient Christians who would not be included in this category made the term "Gnostic" a major feature of their teachings (Clement of Alexandria and Evagrius of Pontus, for example). Moreover, by placing people and texts in such a weighty category based on these two elements, this model exaggerates the importance of these features, singling them out as somehow central to the religious identities of the authors. Surely, however, if one asked the Valentinian teacher Ptolemy or the author of *The Secret Book According to John* what the heart of their teachings were, they would not adduce the creator god or the soul's origin and fate. Rather, they would more likely point to their proclamation of salvation in Jesus and the new way of life this salvation makes possible.

In the end, the problem with any typological method of defining Gnosticism is that it extracts and isolates doctrinal points or general characteristics from complex and often strikingly different mythologies. An evil or ignorant creator god can appear in any number of different creation narratives, with quite different meanings. A scholar may have good reason to study how such a motif functions in different myths, but to create an entire category of religious traditions from such fragmentary and isolated motifs or concepts does not do justice to how people combine myths, rituals, and social institutions to create unique religious subcultures. The proponents of recent typologies may insist that they are creating only a heuristic category and not claiming to define a distinct religion, but the label "Gnosticism" nonetheless lends itself to the kind of reification against which especially King rightly warns. Instead, it would be far better if historians gave up using "Gnosticism" as an interpretive or heuristic category. If we are interested in ancient Christians (or non-Christians) of any stripe who aspire to "mystical knowledge" or who believe that the human soul originated in a transcendent realm or who think that the creator of this world is evil or ignorant, then we should seek out those Christians and simply call them what they were: for example, ancient religious people interested in "mystical knowledge."

But the rejection of the typological approach does not mean that we have to jettison the adjective "Gnostic" altogether: a third group of scholars believes that it is possible to identify an early Christian movement whose members were known properly as "the Gnostics" and who share a distinct mythology and ritual. That is, the "Gnostics" (and perhaps, if we dare, "Gnosticism") can be retrieved as a *social* category, one that corresponds to a group that recognized itself as such—and was so recognized by others. I believe that it is possible to identify and describe such a Gnostic movement without succumbing to the dangers of rigid boundaries, essentializing, and reification that concern scholars today. To fail to explore and reconstruct (as far as we can) the actual religious communities in which ancient Christians arranged themselves would be to neglect the texture of their religious lives and to atomize early Christianity into a series of individual theological projects. That is, even if we must not imagine religious communities as firmly bounded and integrated systems, there remains merit in attempting to explore the subcultures in which religious people found meaning. If we start at the ground level, we can recover something of the myth and rituals of the ancient Gnostics, unburdened by the clichés and stereotypes that have coalesced around "Gnosticism." We can try to get beyond Irenaeus's vision of false *gnōsis*—ironically enough, with his own unwitting help.

# 2

## IDENTIFYING THE GNOSTICS
## AND THEIR LITERATURE

Any effort to identify the Gnostics in antiquity has to begin with Bishop Irenaeus of Lyons. He wrote *Detection and Overthrow of Gnōsis, Falsely So Called,* also known as *Against the Heresies,* around 180. In this work, Irenaeus by no means sought to describe neutrally the various groups of early Christians of his day and their views; rather, he wanted to demonstrate that his version of Christianity was the only true one and that all others were diabolical errors. In the previous chapter we saw that by incorporating all the teachings and groups that he opposed under the single category of "false *gnōsis,*" Irenaeus set the precedent for thinking of ancient Gnosis or Gnosticism as a vast phenomenon made up of numerous sects and schools, whose teachings were extremely diverse and yet somehow all the same. It is this line of thinking that seems to have left modern scholars with one of two options: either "Gnosticism" was indeed a vast ancient religion or type of religion with a variety of representatives, or it did not exist at all.

Irenaeus presents a hostile account of "Gnostics" and other "heretics," and he has led subsequent scholarship down unproductive paths. For these reasons, it may be tempting to set him aside and instead simply read and interpret on their own terms the surviving writings that came from the Christians that he and others like him sought to marginalize. That would be a sensible way of proceeding if Irenaeus could not be trusted at all, but in fact sometimes we are able to confirm his claims and descriptions (as we shall see below). If Irenaeus expected to persuade his readers that his case against competing forms of Christianity was right, then his account of these forms and their relationships to one another could not completely distort the actual situation that his contemporaries could observe. It is probable that the people and texts that Irenaeus describes really existed and that the myths that he summarizes (and ridicules) really circulated, even if he has distorted the doctrines and practices that rival Christians drew from these myths. Irenaeus is the only author of the second century who provides any detailed account of the Christian diversity of his day. Anyone who hopes to reconstruct that diversity must make some attempt to gather some useful information from Irenaeus by separating what may be reliable from the bishop's distortions.

The term "gnostic"—*gnōstikos* in Greek—provides an opportunity for such a project because it was a positive term in antiquity (and remained so even after Irenaeus and other heresiologists had written works disparaging "Gnostics"). It is unlikely that Irenaeus introduced such an affirmative word as a label for Christians that he believed to be wrong and demonically inspired; rather, "Gnostic" must have already been circulating as a term of self-praise. Before Irenaeus wrote in 180 CE, the adjective *gnōstikos* (having to do with *gnōsis*) was not applied to people but to capacities, intellectual activities, or mental operations: a "gnostic" activity or capacity was one that led to or supplied *gnōsis*, that is, knowledge that was not merely practical but theoretical, immediate, even intuitive. Philosophers and other learned persons used the term "gnostic"; it was not a word that ordinary people would use every day.[1] Bentley Layton has compared it to the modern English term "epistemological," which is a learned adjective applied to abstract concepts and the like. To apply it to people or a group of people would sound strange: "the Epistemologicals" or "the Epistemological Association."[2] So, too, it must have sounded odd to call people "Gnostics" and a group of people "the Gnostic school of thought." But this is what we find in early Christian writings, starting with Irenaeus.

We are interested in the term *gnōstikos* (Gnostic), not in the related word *gnōsis* (acquaintance, knowledge). Multiple religious and philosophical movements and teachers claimed to offer *gnōsis*, that is, acquaintance with God and higher truths. The Christian author of *1 Clement* rejoiced that Jesus Christ had brought "immortal *gnōsis*," and he prayed that the blessed person would have "the ability to declare *gnōsis*."[3] The *Letter of Barnabas* refers to Christian teaching as "the *gnōsis* that has been given to us."[4] Neither of these works contains doctrines that either ancient heresiologists or modern scholars would attribute to Gnostics or Gnosticism (rather, they are seen to represent proto-orthodoxy). They illustrate that an emphasis on *gnōsis* cannot be a defining feature of

"Gnosticism," for the claim to provide *gnōsis* was common and expected. To call people *gnōstikoi*, "Gnostics," however, was not common, but innovative.

In this chapter I argue that this new usage came into being with a new social group, people we can call the Gnostics and the Gnostic school of thought (or sect or movement). I describe a method that scholars have developed to use the information that Irenaeus and others provide to collect additional data about this group from surviving ancient literature. The result does not give us much social information about the Gnostics, but it does produce a set of ancient writings that likely originated among a group of people who called themselves and were known as the Gnostics. This group corresponds to those whom modern historians have often called "Sethians" or "Sethian Gnostics." Historians would do well, however, to abandon the qualifier "Sethian," because it does not have a good basis in the ancient sources and its use opens the door to imagining other varieties of "Gnosticism." Instead, we should simply call these Christians (and no others) the "Gnostics." And so, in contrast to the positions of Michael Williams and Karen King, I do not think that we should give up the term "Gnostic" (although I remain leery of "Gnosticism"). On the other hand, I disagree with Birger Pearson, Christoph Markschies, and others who call a wide variety of early Christians and other ancient people "Gnostics." We should recognize the limited nature of the Gnostic school of thought and not amalgamate other ancient teachers and groups with it, creating a wide-ranging entity called "Gnosticism," which not even Irenaeus would recognize.

## The Gnostics as a Specific Group in Irenaeus

In Irenaeus's work we find the first application of the term *gnōstikos* to people, and although he can use the term in a way that seems to refer to a variety of people whose teachings he condemns (as we shall see below), he uses it more than once to refer to a specific, single group of Christians.[5] In Book I of *Against the Heresies,* Irenaeus begins his description of Valentinus by saying that he "adapted the fundamental principles of the Gnostic school of thought to his own kind of system," and he subsequently remarks that on a certain point Valentinus resembles "the Gnostics—falsely so called!—of whom we shall speak further on."[6] And indeed, later in the book, Irenaeus turns to what he calls "a multitude of Gnostics" and describes the myth that "some of them" teach (*AH*

1.29) and then a similar myth that "others" of them teach (*AH* 1.30–31). At the beginning of Book II, when Irenaeus summarizes what he had said in Book I, he once again mentions "the multitude of the Gnostics" and the points on which they disagree (*AH* 2.1.1). In these passages Irenaeus refers to a group of Christians known as "the Gnostics," and although their teachings do not always agree completely, he believes that they have enough social and doctrinal cohesion to be called a *hairesis*. The term *hairesis* originally had a neutral meaning: it designated a "school of thought" or a "sect," but during the second century it acquired a negative meaning for Christians ("heresy"), a development that I shall discuss in greater detail in Chapters 4 and 5. The important point here is that Irenaeus believes that the Gnostics form a specific group that can be differentiated from other groups. In particular, they differ from Valentinus and his school; Valentinus adapted some of the Gnostics' ideas but was not one himself.

Tertullian of Carthage confirms Irenaeus's view that the Gnostics differ from the Valentinians, but he does not see things precisely in the same way as Irenaeus. In two places he mentions the Gnostics and the Valentinians simply in tandem, as two distinct groups.[7] Tertullian had read Irenaeus, and so he could simply be repeating the language of his predecessor. Yet Tertullian certainly has information about the Valentinians that he did not receive from Irenaeus, and so his testimony is not totally dependent on Irenaeus. In fact, he seems to imply that the Valentinians preceded the Gnostics intellectually, rather than the other way around, as Irenaeus would have it. At the end of his treatise *Against the Valentinians,* Tertullian remarks, "And so the sprouting doctrines of the Valentinians have now grown up into the woods of the Gnostics."[8] So Tertullian, too, understood "the Gnostics" to be a specific group, related to but distinct from the Valentinians.

Irenaeus's insistence that the Gnostics are not really gnostic ("falsely so called!"), that is, that their teaching really does not supply acquaintance with God, indicates that even he recognizes *gnōsis* and being *gnōstikos* to be desirable things. Irenaeus does not say that these Christians called themselves Gnostics, but it seems almost certain that they did. Why else would he call this group by such a positive term and by no other? His diction also suggests that "Gnostics" and "Gnostic school of thought" functioned as proper names for the group.

We know that some early Christians did call themselves "Gnostics"—and not always ones that came to be known as heretics. As far as we can tell, the earliest Christian who uses the term "Gnostic" as a positive self-designation in his own writings is Clement of Alexandria. During the last decades of the second century, Clement worked as a teacher and philosopher in one of antiquity's largest and most intellectually vibrant cities. Although he was a younger contemporary of Irenaeus and shared Irenaeus's opposition to Valentinian Christians and others, Clement's spirituality was quite different from that of the bishop of Lyons. Not an ordained member of any clergy, Clement offered instruction in virtue and Christian philosophy to interested persons. He was a kind of Christian sage, who combined the activities and attributes that we would attribute to a teacher and a spiritual director. Those who studied with him, either as individuals or in groups, must have provided him with his financial support. It is in this context that Clement uses the term "Gnostic."

Clement does not claim to be a member of a group called "the Gnostics" or "the Gnostic school of thought," but he does use the term "Gnostic" for the ideal Christian. The Gnostic is the Christian who, through training in virtue and study of Christian writings, has advanced to a high level of acquaintance with God: "Our Gnostic alone—because he has grown up in these Scriptures and because he preserves the correct apostolic and ecclesiastical line of teachings—lives most correctly according to the Gospel. Sent forth by the Lord, he finds the demonstrations that he seeks in the Law and the Prophets. For to my mind the life of the Gnostic is nothing other than deeds and words that follow the tradition of the Lord."[9] In other words, the person who completes a long period of study with Clement, reading the books that he recommends and learning the doctrines that he teaches, can hope to become a Gnostic.

We learn several important things from Clement's use of the term "Gnostic" for the spiritually advanced Christian. First, it was a positive term and not a term of denigration or abuse: Clement assumes that people would want to be known as or claim to be a Gnostic. Second, Clement did not come up with this term on his own; rather, he was claiming for his form of Christian teaching a term that others were using. In the quotation above, Clement pointedly refers to the ideal Christian that his instruction produces as "*our* Gnostic"; elsewhere he refers to "the Gnostic, *properly speaking*," and he calls "falsely named" his competitors who claim to offer *gnōsis* but who really teach falsehoods.[10] He says that the Christians who followed a teacher named Prodicus called themselves Gnostics, even though they certainly were not deserving of the name in his view.[11] (Tertullian also mentions Prodicus as someone whose teachings resemble those of Valentinus, but he does not use the term "Gnostic" for him.)[12] Clement's use of the term emerged from conflict among rival groups of Christians. Certain Christians claimed to be Gnostics, and Clement responded by saying both that their use of this positive term was illegitimate (as Irenaeus did) and that the Christians who follow his teaching are the true Gnostics (as Irenaeus did not). Finally, when speaking of himself and his followers, Clement did not use "Gnostic" as a group name or a sectarian identification, but as a term for the ideal Christian. Similarly, the Stoics called the ideal Stoic "the sage" *(ho sophos)* but did not call themselves "the Sages." Asked to identify their philosophical allegiance, they would have replied "Stoic." So, too, Clement called the ideal Christian "the Gnostic" but identified himself and his followers simply as "Christians."

Clement's evidence suggests that Irenaeus did not come up with "Gnostics" or "Gnostic school of thought" on his own, either; rather, he knew that this group of Christians applied it to themselves. Why would he have granted this term of praise to Christians he considered to be mired in hopeless error? The phrase "Gnostic school of thought" implies that, unlike Clement, these Christians *did* use "Gnostic" to identify themselves as a philosophical or religious movement; they belonged to "the Gnostic school of thought." They were not Platonists or Stoics or Jews, but Gnostics. Did they also call themselves "Christians"? It is difficult to say when certain individuals or groups adopted the term "Christian" (Paul never did), but either the Gnostics must have claimed to be Christians as well or the manifestly Christian content of their teachings made them (false) Christians in Irenaeus's eyes.

Unlike Clement, Irenaeus did not respond by adopting the epithet "gnostic" in some way for his own form of Christianity, but instead he derided the name as fallacious in the case of the Gnostic school of thought, and he repeated it sarcastically in reference to others. The Gnostics, he insists, are "falsely so called," and he derides the Valentinians for trying to be "more perfect than the perfect and more gnostic than the Gnostics" (*AH* 1.11.1, 5). In this latter remark, although he is still using "Gnostics" to refer to a specific group, Irenaeus likens "gnostic" to "perfect," suggesting that the term can be used also as a more generally positive adjective, as Clement did. But Irenaeus uses it in this less precise way sarcastically and so can offhandedly call "gnostics" many Christians who are not members of the Gnostic school of thought but whose teachings are to his mind just as false, pretentious, and overly complicated as those of the Gnostics.

At several points in Books II, III, and IV (*AH*), he concludes lists of heretical teachers with the phrase "and the rest of the gnostics." For example, in Book IV he contrasts the Father of Jesus Christ, who is "the maker of heaven and earth," with the "false father, who has been invented by Marcion, or by Valentinus, or Basilides, or Carpocrates, or the rest of the falsely called gnostics" (*AH* 4.6.4). We can imagine that if he were a modern writer he would put "gnostics" in scare quotes, for the term functions here as a kind of shorthand for "intellectually pretentious but deluded false Christians." In a similar instance in Book II, he speaks of "Saturninus and Basilides and Carpocrates and the remaining gnostics *(gnostici)* who say similar things," and then in the next sentence he mentions "Basilides and all who are falsely called knowers *(agnoti)*, who in fact say the same things under different names" (*AH* 2.31.1). Here Irenaeus uses two different Greek words (now translated into Latin) in these two phrases: *gnostics* in the first sentence is not a proper name for a sect, but can be put in parallel with another (also sarcastically used) term for know-it-alls *(knowers)*.

On the other hand, it seems that at times Irenaeus uses the phrase "the rest of the Gnostics" or "the remaining Gnostics" to denote the specific school of thought that he describes in Book I. For example, Irenaeus claims elsewhere in Book II that his argument can be used "against those who come from Basilides and against the remaining Gnostics, from whom they too [the Valentinians] received the basic elements of emissions and who were refuted in the first book" (*AH* 2.13.8). Here Irenaeus distinguishes the followers of Basilides from the Gnostics he discussed in Book I and whom he identified as the predecessors of the Valentinians. Although his use of the adjective "remaining" or "rest of" may appear to us to mean that Basilides is included in this group, Irenaeus in fact differentiates Basilides from the group that influenced the Valentinians.

In any event, Irenaeus's expanded and sarcastic use of the term "gnostics" for "pretentious, deluded pseudo-Christian intellectuals" does not contradict his use of the term in Book I (and elsewhere) to refer to a specific group of Christians, whose teachings Valentinus adapted and who almost certainly chose the term "Gnostic" for themselves. Their sincere use of this positive epithet for themselves inspired Irenaeus's ironic and sarcastic use of it for other Christians whose teachings he found equally ludicrous and pretentious.

## Collecting Information about the Gnostics

When Irenaeus discusses the Valentinians, the primary targets of his criticism in *Against the Heresies,* he not only describes their teachings but also gives information about them as a group. He tells his readers that they resemble an ancient school, with teachers and disciples, several of whom he names. And they do not separate themselves from other Christians; rather, many of them are members of the same congregations as followers of Irenaeus and his allies, and they try to persuade other Christians to join their study circles. Scholars have found that much of Irenaeus's description of the Valentinians matches what we find in Valentinian sources. Most likely Irenaeus was personally acquainted with Valentinians and had discussed with them their teachings.

Irenaeus does not provide this kind of social information about "the multitude of the Gnostics": he reports only their teachings, which are not entirely consistent. In Book I (*AH*), he assigns certain teachings to "some of them [the Gnostics]" (Chapter 29) and other beliefs to two sets of "others" (Chapters 30 and 31). Irenaeus appears to indicate that these "some" and "others" belong to the single group of "Gnostics," although they hold somewhat different views. But later heresiologists who used Irenaeus's work decided that the bishop was describing three separate sects and assigned to them different names: "Barbēlōites (1.29), "Ophites" (1.30), and "Cainites" (1.31). More variations on these names appeared as authors inherited and adapted what their predecessors wrote. Irenaeus himself, however, used only the term "Gnostics" for the Christians that he describes in Chapters 29–31 of Book I. The teachings that Irenaeus attributes to the Gnostics consist predominantly of, first, mythological descriptions of God, other divine beings, and the creation of the universe and, second, retellings of the Genesis stories of creation, Adam and Eve, and the fall.

Because Irenaeus reports only mythology and biblical interpretation when he describes the Gnostics and gives no information about their organization or leaders, he probably did not know any Gnostics personally but relied on written sources and even hearsay for his information. For example, he claims that he has "collected their writings" on the topic of the creation of heaven and earth by a divine Womb (*AH* 1.31.2). We can identify two of Irenaeus's sources among surviving works from antiquity. First, his report of the cosmological myth that "some" Gnostics teach (*AH* 1.29) is nearly identical to the myth found in the first part of *The Secret Book According to John,* which survives in Coptic translations; second, he names one book produced by "others" of the Gnostics, *The Gospel of Judas* (*AH* 1.31.1). And so the information about the Gnostic school of thought that we can gather from Irenaeus consists of (1) a distinctive myth or sacred story and (2) literary sources that come from the group. These two kinds of information mutually reinforce one another: the *Secret Book* and the *Gospel of Judas* share the same myth with each other and with Irenaeus's report.

We can assign *The Secret Book According to John* (or *Apocryphon of John*) to the Gnostic school of thought based on Irenaeus's evidence. Irenaeus's summary of the myth taught by "some" Gnostics, which runs from a description of the ultimate God to the production of the ignorant creator god and the material universe (*AH* 1.29), parallels the first part of the *Secret Book*. Both tell how the "unnameable Father" or "Virgin Spirit" unfolded into a series of aeons beginning with one called Barbēlō and ending with one named Wisdom. These aeons include Christ and a set of four "luminaries," the fourth of which is Ēlēlēth. The Barbēlō is the aeonic source of salvation. Both Irenaeus and the *Secret Book* tell also how an impulsive act by Wisdom led to the generation of an ignorant, arrogant ruler who created the material universe in which we live. The two accounts differ in some details (for example, the precise names of the four luminaries), but there can be little doubt that Irenaeus had before him some version of the *Secret Book*.

Irenaeus subsequently reports the teachings of "other" Gnostics. They also parallel the subsequent narrative in the *Secret Book,* but much more loosely, and so appear to come from other sources (*AH* 1.30–31). Here the similarities include the name Ialdabaōth for the first ruler, the double creation of Adam and Eve first as nonmaterial beings and subsequently with material bodies, the importance of Adam's son Seth as spiritual ancestor of the saved people, and the depiction of the flood of Genesis 6 as Ialdabaōth's attack on humanity for its devotion to true divinity. In the next chapter I shall discuss the myth that the *Secret Book* and other writings share in some detail, but for now these basic items will serve as the skeleton of "the Gnostic myth."

It is likely that the *Gospel of Judas* to which Irenaeus refers is the *Gospel of Judas* that was discovered in the late twentieth century and first published in 2006, and thus we can assign that book to the Gnostic school of thought as well. In this case, however, there is less certainty than about the *Secret Book*. Irenaeus mentions Judas at the end of his discussion of the Gnostics. Some Gnostics, he says, believe that Adam's son Cain had a divine origin and that biblical characters such as the Sodomites are their spiritual ancestors; the Sodomites and others were attacked by the ignorant creator god, but saved by the divine being Wisdom. As we shall see, the works that likely come from the Gnostics actually identify Seth as the Gnostics' spiritual ancestor and condemn Cain as demonic, but they do confirm what Irenaeus claims about the Sodomites and attacks by the creator god. Irenaeus then turns to the disciple Judas: "And furthermore—they say—Judas the betrayer was thoroughly acquainted with these things; and he alone was acquainted with the truth as no others were, and (so) accomplished the mystery of the betrayal. By him all things, both earthly and heavenly, were thrown into dissolution. And they bring forth a fabricated work to this effect, which they entitle *The Gospel of Judas*" (AH 1.31.1).

It is not clear whether "these things" that Judas knew means only the immediately preceding teachings about Cain and the Sodomites, which do not appear in the fragments of the newly discovered *Gospel of Judas*, or whether Irenaeus is just referring to Gnostic teachings in general. But otherwise, his description of the Gnostics' *Judas* matches the newly discovered work very well. In the *Gospel of Judas*, Jesus reveals only to Judas the true nature of God and the origins of the universe, while the other disciples ignorantly worship the god who created this world and mistakenly think that he is Jesus' father. Judas's betrayal of Jesus appears to be a necessary step toward the final dissolution of the material world and the return of spiritual beings to the higher realm. Irenaeus does not claim that Judas is a hero or a model for true believers in the gospel that he knows, and indeed the character of Judas is ambiguous or even simply negative in the new gospel. Moreover, both Irenaeus's *Judas* and the new gospel are called *The Gospel of Judas*, rather than the expected *The Gospel According to Judas*, like the Gospels of the New Testament and other early Christian gospels. These considerations suggest that the new *Gospel of Judas* is the one that Irenaeus mentions and came from the Gnostic school of thought.

There are, however, some reasons to doubt this identification. Although *The Gospel of Judas* refers to the same myth that Irenaeus attributes to the Gnostics and that appears in *The Secret Book According to John*, its teachings differ from these other two sources in some significant ways. Like the *Secret Book*, *Judas* calls the ultimate divine principle "the great Invisible Spirit," identifies Barbēlō as the divine aeon that is the source of salvation, and speaks of a divine "Self-Originate" with four attendants. Both call the divine paradigm of humanity Adamas and the saved human beings the descendants of Seth, and both give the creator god(s) the names Ialdabaōth and Saklas (among other epithets). In other ways, however, the two works differ: for example, *Judas* seems to give the higher divine beings a more direct role in the creation and organization of the material universe, although it still sees the material realm as flawed and destined for destruction. In *Judas* the important feminine characters of the *Secret Book,* including the Barbēlō, Wisdom, and Eve, play reduced roles. In addition, the *Gospel of Judas* depicts and argues against a fairly well developed, even "mainstream" Christian Church, with a clergy that both claims descent from the original apostles and presides at celebrations of the Eucharist with sacrificial imagery. This picture of Christian life may not match conditions of the middle of the second century, but instead may suit better the more developed Christian churches of the third century, long after Irenaeus.

To my mind, these objections are not conclusive. We should expect some diversity among the representatives of the Gnostic school of thought. After all, Irenaeus asserts that the two works come from different manifestations or branches of the same movement ("some" and "others"). And in fact, we shall find that some of the differences between *Judas* and the *Secret Book* correspond to variations on the myth found in other works. The social conditions that the *Gospel of Judas* implies may reflect only the local situation of the author and his community, not the general situation of Christianity everywhere. Or its organized Church with an apostolic priesthood may merely reproduce the claims of other Christians the author knows and not depict the reality of social life. The similarities between the *Gospel of Judas* and the *Secret Book* are more compelling than their differences. Both writings present their cosmologies as a revelation from Christ or Jesus to one of the disciples known from the New Testament gospels, Judas and John, respectively. They are both Christian; that is, they present their teachings as the true meaning of Christ and the salvation that he brings, just as Irenaeus claims that the Gnostics are a false Christian group. Indeed, the *Gospel of Judas* criticizes other Christians as vehemently as Irenaeus does. I am inclined, then, to attribute *Judas* to the Gnostics of the second century, and yet I recognize that there are reasons to be uncertain about this hypothesis.

Despite its distorted and polemical presentation, the evidence of Irenaeus connects two pieces of ancient literature and, more importantly, the myth that they share to the Gnostic school of thought. This connection finds confirmation from Porphyry (232/3–305), the third-century disciple of the great philosopher Plotinus (205–269/70). Christian heresiologists after Irenaeus also refer to the Gnostics, but in ways that reflect their dependence on Irenaeus's account. Porphyry, in contrast, presents his own independent report.[13] He claims that around 250, while teaching in Rome, Plotinus came into contact with Christians who were "members of a school of thought" and whom Porphyry subsequently identifies as "the Gnostics." Porphyry lists a number of the Gnostics' writings ("revelations"), two of which—*Zōstrianos* and *The Foreigner (Allogenes)*—were found at Nag Hammadi, and another of which—*The Book of Zoroaster*—is excerpted in *The Secret Book According to John*. Unlike the *Secret Book*, which presents a lengthy mythological narrative, *Zōstrianos* and *The Foreigner* describe mystical ascents through the eternal realms to acquaintance with God. The transcendent realms that they describe, however, are those found in the *Secret Book*, with minor variations. *The Foreigner*'s description of the ultimate God, the Virgin Spirit, is nearly identical to that found in the *Secret Book*.

Together, Porphyry and Irenaeus present a coherent description of a "school of thought" *(hairesis)* whose members were known as "the Gnostics." Irenaeus narrates the myth of the Gnostics and names one of their works, the *Gospel of Judas*, which appears to have survived. In addition, the myth that he tells matches that in the surviving *Secret Book According to John*. Porphyry's account of the Gnostics, brief as it is, confirms Irenaeus's assignment of the distinct myth found in the *Secret Book* to the Gnostic school of thought, and it adds three more literary works—*Zōstrianos*, *The Foreigner*, and the excerpted *Book of Zoroaster*—to those that we can attribute to the Gnostics. The five ancient works that Irenaeus and Porphyry associate with the Gnostics do not agree on all points, as Irenaeus suggests and as one would expect for a movement that endured and multiplied for at least a century. Yet they articulate or refer to the same basic story of God, creation, and salvation, which can be called the Gnostic myth. Moreover, these works show signs that they originate in a group with some sense of communal identity, including references to a baptismal ritual, a special group of saved people ("immovable race," "posterity," "the incorruptible race of Seth"), and other Christians as misguided.

At this point it is possible to collect even more information about the Gnostics by looking for other literary sources that contain or assume the

Gnostic myth. Scholars have been able to identify several of these, most of which were discovered at Nag Hammadi. The pioneer in this effort was Hans-Martin Schenke, who already in 1974 argued that a number of ancient works and heresiological accounts, in his words, all "presuppose the same Gnostic system." Because this system gave prominence to Seth as the ancestor of saved human beings, he called the viewpoint that they shared "the Sethian system" and the religious community that they reflected "Gnostic Sethianism." In addition to *The Secret Book According to John*, Schenke included in his text group not only *Zōstrianos* and *The Foreigner*, as we would expect from Porphyry's evidence, but also from the Nag Hammadi discovery *The Revelation of Adam, The Reality of the Rulers, First Thought in Three Forms, The Three Tablets of Seth, The Holy Book of the Great Invisible Spirit*, and three others.[14] As Schenke proposed, scholars usually refer to these works as "Sethian" and to the people who composed them as "Sethians." In 1995, however, Bentley Layton pointed out that the evidence of Irenaeus and Porphyry suggests that we would do better to call them simply "the Gnostics."[15]

Critics of Schenke's work rightly argued that the "Sethian system" is not very systematic: the various works and accounts in Schenke's text group do not always agree on every point.[16] But "system" was a poor choice of words on Schenke's part: what his texts share is not a system of doctrines, but a sacred story or myth. In the case of a myth, some diversity is to be expected. When people in a religious community retell and pass on the group's myth and traditions, they seldom do so without introducing new episodes or characters, eliminating or combining others, and making other revisions. It is up to both adherents and observers to determine when a myth has been altered so much that it has become a different myth and reflects a different religious community. In Irenaeus's opinion, although the Gnostics did not always agree with each other completely—"some" taught certain things, and "others" taught some different things—they still shared the same overall myth and formed a single religious community that he could distinguish from others (including the Valentinians).

This approach to identifying "Gnostics," and hence "Gnosticism," uses the particular myth that Irenaeus attributes to the Gnostic school of thought and that appears in the literature he and Porphyry assign to it to identify additional literature that emanated from that group. This procedure differs from the typological approach that we examined in Chapter 1 because it does not define Gnosticism in terms of abstract doctrines or general attitudes, such as a lower creator god, anthropological dualism, emphasis on mystical knowledge, salvation by *gnōsis,* and the like. Similar doctrines and attitudes can appear in quite different religions and reflect different myths, and members of a religious community may draw from the same myth different doctrinal conclusions. Adherents of the same religious group may argue, for example, about the status of the body in the spiritual life or how salvation is achieved, but they will share an authoritative story to which they will refer in support of their views. Rather than concepts or general moods, it is that story, the community's myth, that we should seek as basic to a religious group's identity. Christians today disagree strongly about a wide range of issues, but they all share the same basic story of the creation, the fall, the incarnation, death, and resurrection of Jesus, and the future kingdom of God. They express and summarize this shared story in statements like the Apostles' and Nicene Creeds. Christians infer strikingly different doctrines from that story, creating at times very different theological systems, and they disagree even about details in the story (for example, the role of Mary, Jesus' alleged descent into hell, and so forth), but it is devotion to that narrative that sets Christians apart from other religious people. The Gnostic Christians of the second and third centuries lived at a time when Christians did not yet share a single story other than that of the Jewish Scriptures (even if some Christians, like Marcion, rejected that story). Rather, they were inventing new stories from the traditions that they had received; the Gnostic myth was one distinctive attempt to tell the story of God and humanity in light of the Jesus event, an attempt sufficiently different from rival Jesus stories to set them apart as a distinct school of thought. In contrast, this myth is completely absent from *The Gospel According to Thomas,* which can be readily understood without any reference to the Gnostic myth. *Thomas* may teach salvation by *gnōsis* and reflect a dualistic anthropology, but it is not Gnostic.

If shared concepts or attitudes are insufficient to assign different texts or teachers to the same religious group, so, too, are simply the same mythic characters or motifs when the overall myth is otherwise not the same. For example, the appearance of Jesus and his mother Mary in the Qur'an does not mean that Islam and Christianity are the same religion, only that they derive from a shared cultural context and that they arose in interaction with one another. By this principle, we are able not only to include certain works in our set of Gnostic texts but also to exclude others that would otherwise appear to be likely candidates. A good example is an untitled work from Nag Hammadi that scholars now call *On the Origin of the World*. Among its prominent characters is Ialdabaōth, the ignorant and arrogant creator god who is a key figure in the Gnostic myth, and it features other characters and incidents with clear parallels in Gnostic works. But in other, more important respects, the myth that it tells differs considerably from what one finds in *The Secret Book According to John* and related books. These differences are so fundamental that most scholars conclude that we are not dealing with a Gnostic work (in the restricted sense that I am advocating). The author of *On the Origin of the World* probably wrote in the early fourth century, and he borrowed from a wide range of earlier Christian literature to create his own myth, which he hoped would demonstrate a particular philosophical point. He shows no interest in the identity or practice of a religious community and was probably not an adherent of the Gnostic school of thought, or if he was, he was not very concerned to maintain its distinctive traditions (at least in this work).

This approach concludes that most of the works that were found at Nag Hammadi are not Gnostic because they lack the Gnostic myth even if some include certain of its characters or motifs in otherwise quite different stories. Most scholars recognize that the works in the Nag Hammadi codices, which were copied in the second half of the fourth century, represent a variety of religious traditions, including Valentinianism (e.g., *The Gospel of Truth* and *The Tripartite Tractate*), Thomas Christianity (e.g., *The Gospel According to Thomas*), and Hermeticism (e.g., *The Discourse on the Eighth and Ninth*). Yet many still understand the hoard of manuscripts to be a "library" of books that come from "Gnosticism." In fact, however, we do not know who the collector or collectors of the Nag Hammadi codices were (despite occasional reports to the contrary), nor is it clear whether the books made up a library when they were created. It may be possible to detect the interests and concerns that motivated someone to include certain works in a single codex and in a certain order.[17] But the interests and religious commitments of fourth-century readers should not be confused with those of the works' authors and earlier readers, who lived in the preceding centuries. Like other manuscripts from antiquity, the codices contain works all of which appealed to the collector(s), but which represent diverse theologies and original social and religious contexts. By the procedure adopted here, we can identify a minority of the works as coming originally from the Gnostic school of thought of the second and third centuries.

This myth-oriented method of collecting works that originated among the Gnostics differs significantly, then, from the typological approach. It does not extract ideas, characters, or motifs from their mythic contexts and then study them in isolation, nor does it rely on general concepts or spiritual attitudes that may flow from any number of different sacred narratives (for example, an emphasis on *gnōsis* rather than faith). Rather, it looks for a shared myth of origins, fall, and salvation (and, we shall see, a shared ritual as well), which could serve to establish and to maintain the unique identity of a distinct religious movement over time.

Scholars debate precisely which ancient works reflect the distinct Gnostic myth and so should be attributed to the Gnostics. For example, Bentley Layton has proposed that the Nag Hammadi work *Thunder: Perfect Intellect* came from the Gnostics because it has close parallels with other works in the text group and with related heresiological accounts, but other scholars have disagreed with him.[18] I have argued that a work that Schenke included in his "Sethian system," the so-called *Untitled Treatise in the Bruce Codex*, should not be considered part of the group because, although it shares some important parallels with Gnostic works, its myth differs too much from what we find in the *Secret Book* and the other writings. It resembles *On the Origin of the World* in this respect.[19] Mark Edwards, rather than following the method developed by Schenke and Layton and followed here, augments the reports in Irenaeus and Plotinus with the testimony of Hippolytus (more on this below). He comes up with a set of Gnostic works that includes not only the ones I have mentioned, but also a *Treatise on the Omega* by Zosimus of Panopolis and the account of the Naassenes given by Hippolytus.[20] Alastair Logan also includes the Naassenes among the Gnostics.[21] Tuomas Rasimus supplements the so-called Sethian works with works that he calls "Ophite," including *On the Origin of the World*, to create a broader, overlapping category that he designates "classic Gnostic."[22] We have seen that some scholars, like me, believe that *The Gospel of Judas* should be included, especially in light of Irenaeus's evidence, but others disagree, pointing to the differences between its cosmology and that of the other Gnostic works.[23] Doubtless there will always be debates about a few individual works, but there is a large scholarly consensus about most of the works in the group.

Debates like this one and the scholarly uncertainty that they indicate do not call into question the existence either of the shared myth or of the Gnostics who adhered to it. Historians typically disagree about whether to assign certain writings to specific individuals and whether to classify specific texts, individuals, and groups as belonging to religious movements. For example, no one doubts that the apostle Paul or the Church Father Athanasius of Alexandria really existed and wrote works that survive today, but scholars disagree about whether to attribute to them some of the works that survive under their names. Moreover, scholars can assign to an ancient author like Evagrius of Pontus works that survive but not under his name or even that bear the name of another person because the style and content clearly indicate that Evagrius was their author. When they discuss the assignment of texts to specific individuals, historians look for a high degree of coherence in style and content; we do not expect the same person to write in strikingly different styles or to hold directly contradictory ideas unless these differences can be persuasively explained. Attributing works to a religious movement that lasted decades or centuries, as the Gnostics did, does not require such a high degree of coherence, but more agreement than we would expect simply for Christian works of the second and third centuries. The ancient identification of the Gnostics as a *hairesis,* a school of thought, suggests that they would have shared key doctrines that they would defend against those offered by other schools, but that they need not have agreed on all points.[24] It is no surprise, then, that scholars differ about how much consistency to expect among the various works of a group like the Gnostics, which is neither a single author nor an entirely separate religion but a movement or school within a wider religious network. At the conclusion of this chapter, I list the works that most scholars attribute to the Gnostic school of thought.

It may be possible to add even more data to our study of the Gnostics by looking for accounts of similar myths in heresiologists other than Irenaeus, but their dependence on Irenaeus and the vague nature of the other sources for their information makes this step more problematic. For example, Bishop Epiphanius of Salamis, a zealous heresy hunter of the fourth century, describes several groups whose myths appear to be variations on that of our Gnostics. Epiphanius gives them several names: "Sethians," "Archontics," "Borborites," and others, as well as "Gnostics." He cites the titles of literary works that these Christians use (a *Gospel of Eve,* for example), but none of them appear to have survived. Most famously, Epiphanius attributes to the Gnostics strange practices, including ritualized sex, abortion, and cannibalism, and he claims to have firsthand knowledge of their licentious behavior.[25] Scholars disagree about whether and how to use this material to understand the Gnostics. It seems most likely that Epiphanius's reports of ritual atrocities are an instance of a general religious tendency to attribute to the Other perverse opposites of one's own rituals,[26] and his accounts of the myths and assignments of them to groups may be his own imaginative attempts to make sense of literary works whose true origins he did not know. There may be some real information to be found in Epiphanius, but in general we are on safer ground sticking to Irenaeus's and Porphyry's accounts and the primary sources that they permit us to gather.

The approach to the Gnostics that I have outlined here has not received the support of most working scholars. Nearly all of them recognize that the works that this procedure collects probably do come from some distinct religious tradition, which they call "Sethianism" or "Sethian Gnosticism." Even the scholars who have been most critical of the category "Gnosticism" accept the hypothesis of such a set of writings with a common myth. Michael Williams, for example, says that the "interconnections" among the Sethian works "cannot be denied."[27] Karen King has carried out an extensive comparison of "Valentinian" and "Sethian" mythologies.[28] Interpreting *The Secret Book According to John,* she invokes other Sethian works to shed light on problems of exegesis and ritual in that book.[29] But King and Williams object to calling the Christians who produced these works (and no others) "Gnostics." Far more scholars, like Birger Pearson and Marvin Meyer, want to include many more works than the ones gathered here under the category "Gnostic" or "Gnosticism."

Because scholars recognize the shared mythology that ties these works together, the most important objections to this procedure focus on the use of the self-designation as Gnostics as the starting point. Critics point out, first, that none of the works that this procedure collects and assigns to the Gnostics in fact claims to come from the Gnostics or the Gnostic school of thought and, second, that Irenaeus and others mention other persons and groups as calling themselves Gnostics.[30] Let us examine each of these objections. I emphasized above that it is unlikely that Irenaeus would have assigned to this group the name "Gnostics" or "Gnostic school of thought." Rather, "Gnostic" was a positive term and so was almost certainly the group's own designation for itself; this self-designation justifies our use of the term for them. It seems strange, then, that none of the literature that is supposed to have come from this group (*The Secret Book According to John* and the other works) uses this term as a means of self-identification. Instead, as we shall see, these works identify the chosen ones, the saved people, with such names as "the immovable race," "the seed of Seth," and "Those People." I agree with Layton's response to this objection:

> The answer lies in the fact that the name Gnostic was the name par excellence of the members of the *hairesis* [school of thought], their most proper name. As such, its function was not to convey information about what they were like, but rather to express their distinctiveness as a group; not to say what they were, but who they were. The claim to supply (or have) *gnōsis* was absolutely banal, but the use of Gnōstikos *as a proper name* was distinctive. Now, the works in the Gnostic mythographic corpus are pseudepigraphic and mythic in literary character, disguising their real author, audience, and place, date, and reason of composition. They do not speak of second- and third-century school controversies (as do the testimonia of Irenaeus, Porphyry, or Epiphanius), but rather of primordial, eschatological, and metaphysical events and relationships. In such compositions, there is no context in which a second-century school name such as Gnōstikos might naturally occur. Thus, the absence of the proper name "Gnōstikos" in the mythographic corpus is not a significant absence.[31]

The Gnostic texts are mythological works that describe the structure of the divine realm, the creation of the universe, and the first generations of humanity, and most of them purport to come not from recent authors but from authoritative figures from the past, such as Adam, Zoroaster, and the apostle John. We should not expect such writings to use terminology that served to identify members of a specific religious or philosophical group in the second century.

Analogies might help to make this point clear. Birger Pearson notes that many scholars (but not all) believe that the community of Jews that lived at Qumran can be identified as the Essenes that observers such as Josephus describe, and yet none of the literature found there identifies its producers or users as Essenes. Instead, the Qumran works, also eschatological or biblical in nature, use terms such as "children of light" to describe saved people.[32] Consider likewise a modern congregation of Lutheran Christians. The sign outside their church building would almost certainly identify the community as "Lutheran," and individual members might answer "Lutheran" to the question, "What religion are you?" in order to distinguish themselves from other Christians. One would probably find, however, that the term "Lutheran" does not appear in many forms of the literature that the community produces and uses (for example, sermons, worship books, biblical commentaries, Sunday School materials). Instead, members of the community call themselves "brothers and sisters," "people of God," "children of God," or just "Christians." Religious groups use different self-designations for different purposes. Especially in situations in which the community wishes to make its message potentially available to a wide range of people and wants to promote the universality of its claims, it will use terms that are more inclusive and less explicitly sectarian. To the extent that "Gnostic" functioned as the name of a specific school of thought, it would have been less desirable to use it in literature that presented the Gnostic message of salvation to all interested persons.

The case of Clement of Alexandria illustrates that the members of the Gnostic school of thought that Irenaeus discusses were not the only ancient Christians who called themselves "Gnostics," and this is a second important objection to this approach to studying ancient Gnostics. Irenaeus reports that the followers of a Christian teacher named Marcellina "call themselves gnostics" (AH 1.25.6). Hippolytus, who wrote his heresiological treatise in the early third century and made use of Irenaeus's work, claims that the Naassenes and the followers of a teacher named Justin (not Justin Martyr) called themselves gnostics.[33] Why then, scholars rightly ask, should we not call these Christians the Gnostics as well but instead reserve the title for Irenaeus's "Gnostic school of thought"? After all, Irenaeus does not say that his "Gnostics" called themselves that (even though I have argued that they almost certainly did). And if multiple and diverse ancient people and groups were calling themselves Gnostics, how can we separate one such group out as the only people to whom we should give the name? Indeed, we have seen that some proponents of the restricted use of "Gnostic" that I advocate include the Naassenes in the Gnostic school of thought, even though their myth as Hippolytus describes it differs considerably from that of Irenaeus's Gnostics.

In response, we should notice that, in contrast to our Gnostics, Irenaeus and Hippolytus identify Marcellina and the Naassenes primarily in other ways. Irenaeus says that Marcellina belongs to the school of Carpocrates, and Hippolytus repeatedly calls the Naassenes the Naassenes. Here is how Hippolytus introduces the Naassenes: "So the priests and promoters of the teaching [that Hippolytus is about to describe] have been first those who have been called Naassenes, so named in the Hebrew language— for the snake is called 'naas'—but subsequently they have called themselves 'Gnostics,' asserting that they alone have acquaintance with the profound matters."[34] Hippolytus suggests that "Naassenes" is the group's primary name, and they later called themselves "Gnostics" as a claim to having unique knowledge. Irenaeus, however, called the group that we are considering only "the Gnostic school of thought," making *that* designation their exclusive one. The phrase "the Gnostic school of thought" indicates a sectarian designation (as in "the Lutheran Church"), comparable to "school of Carpocrates" and "the Naassenes." It seems probable, then, that Marcellina's followers and the Naassenes used the term "Gnostic" as Clement did, as a claim to the achievement of an ideal Christian character, not as the name of their groups. And in fact, Hippolytus tells us that the Naassenes considered themselves "the only true Christians" and shared certain of their teachings only with "the perfect gnostics."[35] Justin's disciples, he says, "call themselves 'gnostics' in their own way, as if they alone have drunk from the amazing acquaintance of the Perfect and Good."[36] Ironically, when Irenaeus and Hippolytus say that people "called themselves" gnostics, this may indicate that the term functions as a secondary claim to perfection rather than as a sectarian self-designation. Perhaps, as in the case of Clement, they used the self-praising epithet "gnostic" in response to its original use by the Gnostic sect. It is not the Gnostics who are really gnostics: we are! The use of the term "gnostic" in this way—as a term for the ideal or true Christian, the one whose acquaintance with God has been perfected, rather than as a sectarian self-designation—continued long after the Gnostic school of thought had probably faded away. In the last decades of the fourth century, the ascetic theologian Evagrius Ponticus called the Christian monk who had reached the most advanced stage of the ascetic life "the Gnostic." Despite the efforts of Irenaeus, Hippolytus, and others, the positive connotation of the term "Gnostic" never disappeared.

By noticing that Irenaeus uses the term *gnostic* not only in a sarcastic or ironic way to refer to any and all "heretics," but also in a precise way to refer to a specific group of Christians, we can begin to gather evidence for the ancient school of thought whose adherents called themselves and were known as the Gnostics. Irenaeus and Porphyry tell us about the myth that the Gnostics taught, and they summarize and even name literature that the group produced. With this information, it is possible to identify from the surviving works of antiquity those that reflect this myth and thus likely came from the Gnostics. We may also be able to identify other groups that Irenaeus and Epiphanius describe as referring to the same school of thought, but at this point things become much less certain. In the outline below, I have summarized the evidence for the Gnostics that this method collects. With each step, the reliability of the procedure lessens, and for my part I am confident using only the information given in sections I, II, and III. As for the works listed under III.B, I am inclined to see the *Gospel of Judas* as coming from the Gnostics and the *Untitled Treatise in the Bruce Codex* as not; I am uncertain about *Thunder—Perfect Intellect.*

A large number of scholars recognize the grouping of texts and testimonies that I have listed as providing evidence for a religious tradition or community in antiquity, and they have come to call this tradition and the texts "Sethian." Fewer scholars, however, have agreed to the larger claim of this chapter: that we can call these texts and the community from which they came "Gnostic," and that we should not use this term as a sectarian title for any other ancient groups or texts. On the one hand, most scholars wish to continue to use the terms "Gnostic" and "Gnosticism" for a wide range of ancient teachers, groups, and texts, including these. On the other hand, critics of this approach wish to avoid the term "Gnostic" altogether or are not persuaded that it is legitimate to give it to this group. Both of these positions have much to commend them, but my approach recognizes what Irenaeus and his colleagues admit, despite their polemical distortions: there really were Gnostics, but not everyone who believed in a lower creator god, attributed cosmic disaster to Wisdom, or offered *gnōsis* of the ultimate God was one of them.

## Evidence for the Gnostic School of Thought

I. Significant descriptions by contemporary observers
   Irenaeus, *Against the Heresies,* Book I, Chapters 29–31 (Layton, *Gnostic Scriptures,* 163–181)
   Porphyry, *Life of Plotinus,* Chapter 16 (Layton, *Gnostic Scriptures,* 182–184)
II. Surviving ancient works attributed to the Gnostics by Irenaeus and Porphyry
   *The Secret Book According to John* (Layton, *Gnostic Scriptures,* 23–151)
   *Zōstrianos* (Layton, *Gnostic Scriptures,* 121–141)

*The Foreigner* (Layton, *Gnostic Scriptures,* 141–148)

*Book of Zoroaster,* excerpted in the long version of the *Secret Book*

*Gospel of Judas* (but see III.B below)

III. Surviving ancient works that reflect the Gnostic myth found in I and II

    A. Works that have wide scholarly agreement

        *The Revelation of Adam* (Layton, *Gnostic Scriptures,* 52–64)

        *The Reality of the Rulers* (Layton, *Gnostic Scriptures,* 65–76)

        *First Thought in Three Forms* (Layton, *Gnostic Scriptures,* 86–100)

        *The Holy Book of the Great Invisible Spirit, or The Egyptian Gospel*
            (Layton, *Gnostic Scriptures,* 101–120)

        *The Three Tablets of Seth* (Layton, *Gnostic Scriptures,* 149–158)

        *Marsanes* (Meyer, *Nag Hammadi Scriptures,* 629–649)

        *Melchizedek* (Meyer, *Nag Hammadi Scriptures,* 595–605)

        *The Thought of Nōrea* (Meyer, *Nag Hammadi Scriptures,* 607–611)

    B. Works that scholars dispute

        *Gospel of Judas* (Meyer, *Nag Hammadi Scriptures,* 755–769)

        *The Thunder: Perfect Intellect* (Layton, *Gnostic Scriptures,* 77–85)

        *The Untitled Treatise in the Bruce Codex*[37]

IV. Reports of other groups that may reflect the Gnostic myth

        Irenaeus, *Against the Heresies,* Book I, Chapter 24, Sections 1–2
            (Satorninos) (Layton, *Gnostic Scriptures,* 159–162)

        Epiphanius, *Against Heresies,* Chapters 25–26 (Gnostics or
            Borborites), Chapter 39 (Sethians), Chapter 40 (Archontics)
            (Layton, *Gnostic Scriptures,* 185–214)

# 3

## THE MYTH AND RITUALS OF THE GNOSTIC SCHOOL OF THOUGHT

The Gnostic myth was a bold attempt to explain the origin and fate of the universe and to proclaim human salvation through a combination of the Jewish Scriptures, Platonist mythological speculation, and (it seems) revelatory meditations on the structure of the human mind. The somewhat different narrations of the myth often strike the modern reader as exceedingly complex, even comically so. Important divine characters have strange names—Barbēlō, Ēlēlēth, Ēphēsēkh, and others—and relate to one another in obscure ways. Highly philosophical vocabulary— jargon, really—fills Gnostic writings. Appreciation of these works as religiously compelling, and thus of the Gnostic school of thought as an attractive religious option among Christian groups, requires that we look for the message of salvation that the Gnostic myth means to communicate (even if we cannot figure out whether, say, in *The Holy Book of the Great Invisible Spirit* the Moirothea is indeed the same character as Plēsithea).

Although the sheer intellectual enjoyment of cosmological speculation must have contributed to the exuberant complexity of Gnostic mythmaking, we must not imagine that the Gnostics were just playing mind games. In recent decades scholars have recognized that ancient philosophical schools did not engage in philosophical discourse about the nature of God and other high doctrines for purely intellectual reasons; rather, they were communities in which individuals learned a way of life based on shared principles and teachings. Philosophy sought to make people more virtuous, in fact, happier, for ancient intellectuals agreed that no person could be truly happy without being virtuous.[1] There is no reason to think that the Gnostic school of thought differed from its contemporaries in this respect. We can assume that their teachings also had a therapeutic purpose: to reconnect the human intellect with the source of its being and to ameliorate its condition of attachment to the body and its passions. For the Gnostics, as for their fellow Platonists, the intellect provided the link between humanity and the divine because our intellect is modeled after and provides a means to connect with the intellect of God. And so the Gnostic myth provides a map, so to speak, of the divine intellect, and it explains how, despite our life in the body and opposition by demonic powers, our intellect still provides us with the opportunity to contemplate God. Divine revelation in Christ made this message available, and Gnostic ritual provided a basis for mystical ascent to knowledge of God.

This chapter surveys the key features of the Gnostics' myth and their rituals of baptism and mystical ascent. It discusses also how Gnostics differentiated themselves from other Christians and recent theories as to the origin and social character of the Gnostic sect. I do not attempt here a detailed discussion of any of these topics; rather, I wish to situate the basic teachings of the Gnostics within their ancient context and to discern the compelling features of their message. Given how little evidence survives, there is much that we will never be able to know about the Gnostics, but when one examines the evidence that comes from the Gnostic school of thought on its own, it is possible to discover an emphasis on saving knowledge of the divine, made possible through Christ. What often passes as the primary characteristics of "Gnosticism"—dualism, alienation, esotericism, and the like—do not appear nearly as central as the Gnostics' conviction that God had acted to save people from the machinations of the evil forces that surrounded them.

## God and the Divine Realm

According to the Gnostics, the ultimate God—"the Father of the entirety" or "the Invisible Spirit"—is unknowable and beyond description. One should not even think of the Invisible Spirit as divine because "it is superior to deity" (*Ap. John* II 2:35–36). On the one hand, only negative adjectives can describe the Invisible Spirit—immeasurable, invisible, unlimited, and so on—but even these are not negative enough: "It is not corporeal, it is not incorporeal . . . Indeed, no one can think of it" (*Ap. John* II 3:22–26). On the other hand, because it is the source of all that is, one can say some things: "It is life, as bestowing life. It is blessed, as bestowing blessedness. It is acquaintance, as bestowing acquaintance."

But the Invisible Spirit does not have any of these characteristics; rather, it bestows them on all existing things less than itself (*Ap. John* II 4:3–8). One Gnostic author actually postulates a divine entity even higher than the Invisible Spirit, the Unknown Silent One (*Mar.* 4:19–24).

Despite the Invisible Spirit or Father of the entirety's remote serenity, it is essentially an intellect, and so its nature is to think, and this thinking results in the devolution of God into an "entirety" with a complex structure of "aeons." The aeons are simultaneously actors, places, extents of time, and modes of thought. They mostly have names of ideal qualities, abstractions, or mental operations, such as Intelligence, Truth, Form, Afterthought, and Wisdom. The aeons that make up the entirety result from the Invisible Spirit's knowledge or thought of itself. They are its thinking or its intellect, in all its complexity. They form also a spiritual realm, the equivalent of Plato's realm of ideal forms. In Plato's view, the material universe in which we live is an imperfect but very good copy of a spiritual realm of ideas or ideal forms that alone are real—that is, unchanging and eternal. Likewise for the Gnostics, only the entirety that the aeons constitute is truly real and eternal; the material world is a flawed imitation of the entirety and destined to perish.

Foremost among the aeons is the second principle, "the image of the perfect Invisible Virgin Spirit" (*Ap. John* II 4:34–35), which is the most immediate emanation from the ultimate God. The potential for any lower being to have *gnōsis* of the first principle rests in this aeon, which is called Forethought and, more obscurely, the Barbēlō.[2] The Barbēlō itself can have constituent aeons. Usually there are three of these, called concealed, first-manifest, and self-originate. If the Invisible Spirit is the ultimate font of humanity and our salvation and yet cannot be named and described, then the Barbēlō is the more immediate source of which human beings can speak. In *The Gospel of Judas,* Judas says to Jesus: "You have come from the immortal aeon of the Barbēlō. But as for the one who sent you"—that is, the Invisible Spirit—"I am not worthy to say his name" (35:17–21). After the first principle and the Barbēlō, different versions of the myth populate the divine realm in different ways, albeit with some recurring motifs, such as the number 24. But they all share the view that ultimately there is one single reality, yet the magnificent complexity of this ultimate reality expresses itself in a multifaceted divine realm of aeonic emanations.

Several divine characters or structures appear in similar ways even within narrations of the myth that otherwise differ, suggesting that they lay at the heart of what Gnostics saw as distinctive about their teachings about God. For example, nearly all feature a triad of father, mother, and son at a very high level of the godhead. In *The Secret Book According to John*, the Barbēlō conceives by the gaze of the first principle and begets a spark, the Self-Originate or Christ. Unlike other aeons, which emanate by becoming "disclosed," Christ is "the only-begotten" of the Father and the Barbēlō, who are then his father and mother (*Ap. John* II 6:10–18). According to *First Thought in Three Forms*, the "sound" of the Barbēlō "exists as three compartments: Father, Mother, Son—a voice existing imperceptibly" (37:20–23). This motif becomes even more prominent in *The Holy Book of the Great Invisible Spirit*, which contains at least six triads of father, mother, and child, beginning with the Invisible Spirit, the Barbēlō, and their "thrice-male child."[3] Although it can take different forms, a family of father, mother, and son lies at the center of the Gnostic conception of the divine. Even if Gnostic writers had a negative view of sexuality, they nonetheless saw the human family as "an imperfect image of divine reality."[4]

In several versions of the myth, the character designated "Self-Originate" or "Christ" or both is a central figure within the entirety, functioning as a kind of pivot from the supreme beings the Invisible Spirit and the Barbēlō to the remaining aeons. Four aeons called luminaries often attend or surround this figure. For example, we have met the Self-Originate or Christ of *The Secret Book According to John*, whom the Father and the Barbēlō beget. According to this work, "the invisible Virgin Spirit established the Self-Originate as true god over the entirety, and subordinated to it [the Self-Originate] all authority and the truth that was in it [the Spirit]" (*Ap. John* II 7:22–26). In *First Thought* the aeons praise Christ, who is "the only-begotten" and "the perfect child" and who establishes four eternal realms and their luminaries (38:16–39:12). *Zōstrianos* calls the lowest level of the Barbēlō "the self-originate aeon" and places the four luminaries within it (*Zōs.* 19:6–16; 29:1–20). *The Gospel of Judas* calls the Self-Originate, as it does many of the divine beings, "a great angel" and "the god of light"; it is attended by four angels, and it brings into existence the lower aeons (47:16–48:21). The Self-Originate or Christ serves as the transitional figure from the primal triad of the Invisible Spirit, the Barbēlō, and himself, to the numerous aeons that make up the entirety of the divine realm.

The four luminaries that attend the Self-Originate (along with the archetypal human beings that often dwell with them) are perhaps the most distinctive characters in Gnostic myth. In the *Secret Book* the four luminaries—Harmozēl, Ōroiaēl, Daueithai, and Ēlēlēth—stand before the Self-Originate or Christ, and each of these is actually the lead aeon in a set of four aeons (*Ap. John* II 7:30–8:28). These four luminaries, bearing the same names, appear also in *First Thought,* where they receive additional names and are called "the eternal realms." Here, too, they are closely linked with Christ, who "established" them while they are said (perhaps mistakenly) to have "engendered" him (38:30–39:13). The luminaries play a similar role in the *Holy Book,* which gives them consorts, attendants, and even consorts to their attendants (IV 63:8–65:5). As we have seen, *The Gospel of Judas* calls the Self-Originate "a great angel," and so too are his four attendants: "And for his sake four angels came into being from another cloud, and they came into being for the attendance of the angelic Self-Originate" (47:21–26). One or more of the four luminaries appear in other works as well. If the Self-Originate or Christ serves as a kind of pivot between the Invisible Spirit and the Barbēlō on the one hand, and the subsequent aeons on the other, the four luminaries provide the focal structure for the subsequent aeons, which in the *Secret Book* number twelve.

More significantly, the four luminaries are key aeons because they provide realms or dwelling places for the divine archetypes of ideal humanity, which are transcendent versions of the earliest and later human beings. If, as Genesis claims, human beings were made according to a divine "likeness" (Genesis 1:26), and if, as Plato teaches, our world is a copy of the spiritual world, then it makes sense that the entirety would include divine archetypes of human beings. These include Adamas, the heavenly archetype of Adam, who resides with or in Harmozēl, and his son Seth, who resides with or in Ōraoiaēl. These first two archetypes are clear enough, but the third and fourth archetypes are collective and somewhat more obscure. The seed or posterity of Seth resides with or in Daueithai. This seed of Seth probably refers to the descendants of Seth who lived during the primeval era of the early chapters of Genesis, because the fourth luminary, Ēlēlēth, plays host to the archetypes of people who appear to be saved human beings of later historical periods, perhaps the contemporary Gnostics themselves (*Ap. John* II 8:28–9:24). According to the *Holy Book,* "the offspring of the great Seth repose" in Daueithai, while "the souls of the offspring repose" in Ēlēlēth (*Gos. Eg.* III 65:17–22; IV 77:16–20). The *Secret Book* describes the latter group as "those who were not acquainted with the fullness and did not repent at once, but held out for a while and then repented." Unlike the posterity of Seth, they were "engendered beings" who nonetheless "glorified the Invisible Spirit" (*Ap. John* II 9:19–24). Perhaps these souls are "engendered" as offspring through the ritual of baptism, which I shall discuss below. Finally, in *The Reality of the Rulers*, it is Ēlēlēth who appears to the heroine Nōrea. Nōrea's "offspring," the luminary tells her, "exist immortal in the midst of dying humankind," but they will not appear until "after three generations," when "the true human being, within a modeled form, reveals the existence of [the spirit of] truth, which the Father has sent" (*Hyp. Arch* 96:19–97:1). This may be a reference to the incarnation of Jesus. All of these passages suggest that Ēlēlēth is the luminary of the archetypes of the contemporary Gnostics and other saved human beings. And so there are four divine archetypes of humanity: Adam (Harmozēl), Seth (Ōraoiaēl), the primeval descendants of Seth (Daueithai), and the contemporary Gnostics, the present-day seed of Seth (Ēlēlēth).

The structure of the entirety may be complicated—there are usually many more characters than I have named here—but it possesses a serene stability, sometimes based on gender complementarity: most of the aeons exist in male-female pairs that subordinate femininity to a masculinity that is purported to be beyond gender. On the one hand, as perfect, uncreated emanations of the ultimate principle, the aeons do not possess gender, or they exist beyond gender. The Barbēlō, for instance, is called "the mother-father" and "the thrice-androgynous name" (*Ap. John* II 5:6–9). On the other hand, in Greek many of the aeons' names have a grammatical gender—"truth," for example, is *alēthē*, a feminine noun— and so are referred to with feminine pronouns. And thus they seem, at least superficially, to have a gender, and some versions of the myth either assert or hint that the aeons have "consorts" of the other gender. Both the *Secret Book* and Irenaeus report that intellect (masculine) is paired with prior acquaintance (feminine), and will (masculine) with eternal life (feminine)(*Ap. John* II 7:11–13; *AH* 1.29.1). The pairing of aeons and the use of androgyny as a term of praise suggest a complementarity of the genders, which gives the entirety stability and, it might seem, a measure of gender equality. Nonetheless, the ultimate principle still seems to be a "father," and the Barbēlō is praised not only as "the thrice-androgynous name" but also as "thrice-male" (II 5:8), a term of praise that appears more than once in Gnostic works. One might say that in Gnostic myth the divine transcends gender by incorporating femininity into a more basic or dominant masculinity.

In at least one version of the myth, it is the violation of gender complementarity by the aeon Wisdom that precipitates the creation of a flawed material world. According to the *Secret Book,* Wisdom is the last of the twenty-four aeons and thus the most distant, so to speak, from the Invisible Spirit. When Wisdom (in Greek, *Sophia*) produced a thought on her own, without the consent of her male consort, the result was an imperfect thought or pseudo-aeon, the first "divine" being that does not belong to the entirety of immortals. Wisdom cast this misshapen product of her thinking outside the entirety and named it Ialdabaōth. Ialdabaōth, also called Saklas and other names, is the misguided creator and ruler of this material universe, that is, the God of Genesis. Similarly, *The Reality of the Rulers* claims that Wisdom "wanted to create something, alone without her partner" (*Hyp. Arch.* 94:6–7), and the result was Ialdabaōth. In this view, then, Wisdom disrupts the gendered balance among the aeons of the entirety by thinking or creating independently, without her male consent, and this error results in the flawed created order. Here the entirety appears to have held within itself the potential for its own undoing: the increasing distance of the succeeding emanations from the first principle makes lack of harmony increasingly possible, to the point that such disharmony becomes actual when Wisdom attempts to think on her own. The transition from the spiritual entirety of blessed aeons to the material world of creatures appears to be a mistake, something that divine providence did not intend and, as we shall see, a problem that must be rectified. Wisdom later repents of her error and is restored to the community of aeons, even elevated to a higher position.

Other Gnostic works take a more positive view of the origins of the material universe, even though they still do not see it as desirable in comparison to spiritual reality; likewise, they do not cast Wisdom in as negative a light. For example, the *Holy Book* has the luminary Ēlēlēth initiate the production of a material universe and its god by announcing, "Let something rule over chaos and Hades" (*Gos. Eg.* III 56:22–25). Here Wisdom plays an important role in the generation of matter and the emanation of rulers over it, but she does so neither solely on her own initiative nor as a mistake, but in concert with other immortal beings. *First Thought in Three Forms* seems to include elements of both of these views: on the one hand, it calls Wisdom "the innocent one," and Ialdabaōth just appears as "the great demon," without any error on Wisdom's part; on the other hand, it portrays the higher aeons as forgiving Wisdom for the production of Ialdabaōth.[5] *The Gospel of Judas* likewise does not mention Wisdom at all in the generation of Ialdabaōth; rather, Ialdabaōth appears to come into being by an act of divine will. Here "Saklas" names yet another lower ruler (51:8–15). The Gnostics, then, held a range of views about the origin of the material universe and its ruler, but they all agreed that Ialdabaōth, the god of this world, is arrogant and ignorant, and his realm is one of darkness and corruption.

The myth, then, emphasizes the transcendence of the ultimate God and the corresponding unfolding of God into lower, mediating divine principles, the lowest of which does the work of creating the material universe. These ideas are not unique to the Gnostics; rather, they are at home in the discourse of Middle Platonism, a philosophical movement represented by figures like Philo of Alexandria, who lived in the first century, and Alcinous, Numenius, and Justin Martyr, philosophers of the second century. Philo was a Jew; Justin, a Christian; and Alcinous and Numenius, adherents of traditional Greek and Roman religions—but they all agreed that it is too simple to identify the god who created the world in which we live with the ultimate divine principle. These thinkers looked for guidance on the world's origin to Plato's dialogue *Timaeus,* in which a divine being called "the craftsman" (demiurge) creates the visible universe as a copy of the eternal forms. The craftsman creates lower gods, who then assist him, and the universe that he creates and in which we live is the best possible image of the perfect spiritual world.

In the *Timaeus* Plato does not mention a god that is higher or more abstract than the craftsman, but later Platonists concluded that there must be such a higher God. After all, if the craftsman created this world in imitation of a higher one, who created the higher world? Moreover, in another dialogue, *Parmenides,* Plato speaks of an ultimate divine principle, "the One," which is beyond any description and cannot be said even to exist in the way that we normally think of existing.[6] The craftsman of the *Timaeus,* as divine and powerful as he is, does not appear to be as remote and abstract as the One. During the first and second centuries CE, intellectuals, especially admirers of Plato's thought, became increasingly sensitive to the distance between the changing material nature of our world and the ideal of an unchanging, wholly spiritual existence, of which the One would be an extreme representative. If the ultimate God is utterly transcendent, unchanging, and immaterial, as the ideals of Plato suggested, then some sort of mediating divine principle(s) between that God and this created order appeared necessary.

Ancient thinkers drew on a variety of traditions to understand this mediation, and they employed several metaphors to describe the unfolding of the ultimate God. In addition to Plato's works, Philo turned to the Jewish Scriptures to understand the nature and complexity of God. The ultimate God, he believed (and echoing the *Parmenides*), is best understood simply as "the one that is," as indeed God said to Moses from the burning bush: "I am that I am" (Exodus 3:14). Philo concluded, then, that the divine names that appear in the Bible, like "God" and "Lord," must refer not to God himself, but to powers or aspects of God, in the cases of "God" and "Lord" his creative and ruling faculties, respectively. God is therefore somehow not just one, but three. This is why God appeared to Abraham by the oaks of Mamre in the form of three men (Genesis 18:1–2). Most people can perceive only the lower powers of God, but the purest and most learned human intellect might be able to "apprehend the Existent alone by itself."[7]

"God" and "Lord" are not the only powers of God that Philo identified; they are merely the "senior" ones. According to Genesis, God created the universe by speaking: "Then God said, 'Let there be light'; and there was light" (Genesis 1:3). It is God's voice that brings the world into existence. Thus, Philo designates as the Word *(logos)* of God the divine principle that mediates between the ultimate God and the created world. The Father of All has established "his chief messenger," the Word, "to stand on the border and separate the creature from the Creator."[8] Jews like Philo also saw God's Wisdom as a mediating, creative figure. In Proverbs, Wisdom, a feminine figure, claims that God created her first among all things, and she assisted him in the creation of the universe (8:22–31). "I came from the mouth of the Most High," Wisdom announces in Sirach (24:3), laying the foundation for Jews and Christians to identify Wisdom with the Word of God.

The Christian teacher Justin Martyr, whom we shall study at greater length in the following chapter, agreed that a lower divine principle mediates between God and the creation. He not only identified God's Wisdom with God's Word, but identified both with Christ. Christians had, of course, already made this move: Paul called Christ God's Power and Wisdom (1 Corinthians 1:24), and one of his disciples claimed that "in him [Christ] all things in heaven and on earth were created" (Colossians 1:16). The Gospel of John identified Christ as God's Word, through whom "all things came into being" (John 1:1–3). Following these precedents, Justin agreed with the Gnostics and Philo that the ultimate God, the Father, is really unnameable: titles like "Father" and "God" and "Lord" just refer to what God does, not who God is.[9] And so the ultimate God has a Son, "another god," the Word *(logos)*, who gives order to the universe and reveals the ultimate God to human beings.[10] The Father and the Son are "distinct in number, but not in mind."[11] Because the Father is remote from us, it is the Word who appeared to people like Abraham and Moses in the Bible. Not only this, but God has another emanation, the Spirit. Philo and Justin would have agreed that it was not the ultimate God who in Genesis appears to people and mediates divine revelation, but some lower emanation of him.

Philosophers like Alcinous and Numenius did not use the Jewish Bible as Philo and Justin did, but they, too, discerned mediating principles between the highest God and the created world. Numenius distinguished between the craftsman god, whom most human beings are able to recognize, and "the first God" or "first mind," who not merely participates in the Good, but is the Good; the first God is associated not with becoming, but with pure being.[12] Like the Gnostics, Alcinous taught that God's thinking constitutes the realm of true spiritual reality: "The forms are eternal and perfect thoughts of God."[13] He, too, distinguished between "the primal God" or "primary intellect" and a lower god he called "the intellect of the whole heaven." Alcinous described the ultimate God in terms very similar to those in which the Gnostic works *The Secret Book According to John* and *The Foreigner* describe the Invisible Spirit: "He is neither genus, nor species, nor differentia, nor does he possess any attributes," and so on.[14] Moreover, Alcinous agreed with the Gnostics that the ultimate God does not directly rule the universe in which we live, rather that multiple "other divinities, the daemons, whom one could also term 'created gods,'" administer the world beneath heaven.[15]

In comparison to these thinkers, the Gnostics appear to stand out for two reasons: their divine mediating principles are numerous and complex, and their craftsman god is ignorant and even malicious. Certainly, the Gnostics' divine entirety is far more complicated and thickly populated than what Philo, Numenius, or Alcinous imagined, but their numerous eternal beings only extend closer to the ultimate God the multiplicity of divinities that characterized all ancient views of the cosmos. No ancient person (even one who was a Jew or Christian) was a monotheist in our sense, that is, someone who believes that one and only one God exists. Instead, ancient "monotheists" simply believed that a single High God stood atop a hierarchy of gods, daemons, and other spiritual beings.[16]

Neither were the Gnostics alone in their multiplication of divine aspects of the ultimate God. Christians such as Basilides and the Valentinians also imagined a complex godhead with multiple aeons, and like the Gnostics, they concluded that the god who created this world was more imperfect than Plato's craftsman god. The Gnostics' understanding of God was certainly distinctive, but it lay within the range of speculative thought during their time. And finally, the complexity of the Gnostics' God matches the complexity of the human mind, which reflects God's rationality. If human beings are to understand their true nature, reform their lives, and achieve the knowledge of God for which they were created, then they can only benefit from as detailed a map of the divine intellect as possible.

The Gnostics are sometimes called dualists, but this can be a misleading description of their thought. To be sure, the Gnostics drew a sharp contrast between the material world in which we live and the spiritual realm of the immortal aeons. Our world changes, subjects us to fate, suffering, and death, and obscures our knowledge of God; the matter that constitutes it is destined for ultimate destruction. True reality, in contrast, does not change, exists in stability and harmony, and is eternal. But strictly speaking, dualists posit two eternal and opposed ultimate principles, from which the opposing realms of matter and spirit originate, and the Gnostics do not teach this. Ultimately, there is only one Invisible Spirit, and everything that exists has its origin in it. Indeed, the Gnostics are even less dualistic than Plato, who appears to have imagined that a formless material principle, the receptacle of being, always existed alongside God and constituted the stuff to which the craftsman gave order. The Gnostics, in contract, imagined even the material world as originating from the entirety (at least in the works in which they are explicit on this point). This lower universe is not completely foreign to the divine realm; rather, the entirety is its source.[17] And so the myth does not suggest that Gnostics should utterly "reject" the material world (how could they?), but that they should understand that this world came into being for a reason even if it is ultimately not humanity's true home.

## The Material World, Biblical History, and the Possibility of *Gnōsis*

The unfolding of the single divine reality into the complex structure of the entirety took place before the beginning of time, or rather, it happens outside of time, before or apart from Genesis 1:1. Clues to this process appear in the Bible, however: it seems that the mythic unfolding of God and the error of Wisdom take inspiration from the first three chapters of Genesis as well as from Plato. For example, Wisdom is certainly a kind of Eve figure—sinner, penitent, and mother.[18] Genesis comes more explicitly into view as the Gnostics describe the creation of this world and the first human beings. In contrast to the spiritual entirety, the Gnostics understood this world to be "corporeal darkness, . . . animate chaos and desirous femininity" (*Zōs.* 1:11–13), yet the enlightened person could experience divine stability and eternity through a process of mystical contemplation, which we shall explore below. Such first-hand acquaintance *(gnōsis)* with the ultimate, indeed sole, reality could only be a rare and fleeting experience for those few intellects able to transcend their present condition of imprisonment in a material body, which was troubled by the passions and enslaved to fate in a universe controlled by demonic powers.

The portion of Gnostic myth most obviously based on the Jewish Bible explained how the human intellect found itself in this unhappy situation, how the potential for reunion with the divine has persisted from the origins of time, and how the immortal beings have acted to rescue human beings in Jesus. Gnostics read the opening chapters of Genesis as a confused account—muddled by its uncomprehending author, Moses—of how the divine potentiality came into this world and how it has survived the various attempts of the demonic forces to seize or eliminate it. As we have seen, the Gnostics differed on precisely how the material universe came into being and how Wisdom was involved in it, but in any case the result was a distorted thought, a contemptible false version of divinity named Ialdabaōth and identified as both the "craftsman" *(demiourgos)* of Plato's *Timaeus* and the "God" of Moses' Genesis. While Plato's craftsman god created this world as the best possible copy of the eternal forms, Ialdabaōth formed the material universe as a highly imperfect copy of the spiritual entirety of which he had a dim memory. He exemplifies the self-deception of ignorant beings, vainly announcing to all who would listen, "For my part, I am a jealous god. And there is no other god apart from me" (see Exodus 20:5; Deuteronomy 4:24; 6:15; Isaiah 45:5). As a Gnostic author remarked, the god of Israel (that is, Ialdabaōth) here unwittingly testifies to the existence of a higher God, "for if no other one existed, of whom would he be jealous?" (*Ap. John* II 13:5–13).

The depiction of the god of Genesis as ignorant, foolish, and even malicious may be the feature of Gnostic mythology that most offended other ancient Christians and still puzzles modern readers. We have already noted that philosophically inclined Jews and Christians agreed that the creator god in Genesis resembled the craftsman god of Plato's *Timaeus* and was not the highest God, but the Gnostics took a much less positive view of this divine being. Their view most likely developed from passages in the Bible that portray God as ignorant and wrathful. The god of Genesis, after all, walks in an earthly garden and must ask where Adam is (Genesis 3:8–9); he concludes that his creation of humanity and animals was a mistake and decides to destroy all people, except for a single family and a few beasts (6:5–22); and he later annihilates entire cities by raining sulfur and fire down upon them (19:24–25). Such passages troubled many pious readers of the Bible in antiquity: some learned interpreters argued that these events are not literally true, but have spiritual meanings; others attributed these actions to a lower, less perfect manifestation of God, his "presence" or his "word."[19] The Gnostics solved this problem simply: this god is as ignorant, vain, and hostile to human beings as he appears. Therefore, he must not be truly divine, not truly God, but Ialdabaōth. Moses failed to recognize this fact, and thus Genesis, which he wrote, provides only a partially reliable account of creation, Adam and Eve, and their progeny.

Despite his imperfection, Ialdabaōth was able to create the universe thanks to the "great power" that he took from his mother Wisdom (*Ap. John* II 10:20–21). Wisdom's power generates hostility between human beings and Ialdabaōth, and the return of this power to the entirety is the goal of divine providence. Ialdabaōth does not rule the universe alone, but leads a set of demonic powers, called rulers, authorities, and the like. The Gnostics found the number, names, and characteristics of these rulers grimly fascinating, and one Gnostic author devoted his treatise to demonstrating "the reality of the rulers" and their threat to human beings, about which Paul warned Christians in his letter to the Ephesians: "Our contest is not against flesh and blood; rather, the authorities of the world and the spiritual hosts of wickedness" (Ephesians 6:12; *Hyp. Arch.* 86:20–27). *The Secret Book According to John* provides the most extensive discussion of the rulers and lists of their names. Here the rulers are heavenly authorities, associated with the stars and planets, and astrological fate constitutes much of their power over human beings. The rulers thwart our potential virtue and knowledge of God by controlling our choices astrologically. One version of the *Secret Book* preserves an excerpt from the otherwise lost *Book of Zoroaster*, which names the ruler who made each part of the human body, perhaps so that Gnostics can bind or invoke the ruler when they need to heal that body part.[20] Knowing the names and hierarchies of the rulers may have been one way for Gnostics to resist their evil influences.

The power that Ialdabaōth took from Wisdom came into humanity when Ialdabaōth created Adam and was tricked into blowing his spirit into him. Humanity's resulting upright stature and aspirations toward the higher reality brought it into conflict with the cosmic rulers. The exact sequence of events at this point varies among the Gnostic works that retell the story of Adam and Eve, although they all base their accounts on Genesis. Gnostic authors, however, do agree that the original human being was created in two steps, first spiritually and then materially. First, Ialdabaōth and the rulers create a spiritual human being in imitation of the image of the divine human being that is displayed to them from the entirety above. This "animate" Adam is made, as Genesis would have it, "in the image of God" (Genesis 1:27). But subsequently the rulers consign this spiritual human being to a material body, and they create Eve as Adam's partner, or they divide the originally androgynous human being into the male Adam and the female Eve. The idea of such a two-stage creation of humanity is not unusual among early Jewish and Christian authors, for it helped them to make sense of the two accounts of the creation of humanity found in the first two chapters of Genesis (1:26–30; 2:4–25). Modern biblical scholars hypothesize that the author(s) or compiler(s) of Genesis combined two originally separate accounts of creation, but ancient interpreters did not have recourse to this theory. Many of them, like the Gnostics, concluded that Genesis 1 recounts the creation of an androgynous, perhaps entirely spiritual human being ("male and female"), whom God subsequently divided into male and female beings with material bodies ("dust").[21] Despite this agreement on humanity's double creation, Gnostic works differ in how they trace the survival of the divine power through this process of creation and subsequent "fall."

In *The Secret Book According to John*, the entrance of Wisdom's power into Adam enables him to stand upright. Adam's upright stature indicates his attraction to higher, spiritual realities, which brings him into conflict with Ialdabaōth and the rulers who created him. Because Adam lives in a physical body whose passions obstruct virtue and knowledge of

God, and because the rulers seek to prevent his acquaintance with the divine, Adam requires help from the entirety. He receives this help in the form of luminous Afterthought, a manifestation of Wisdom, who instructs and enlightens human beings. This female revelatory principle becomes active and manifest when Eve is created and separated from Adam. The rulers attempt to rape the spiritually endowed Eve, but the spiritual principle abandons Eve's material body before they do so, and their intercourse with the merely fleshly Eve results in the births of Cain and Abel. Intercourse between Adam and Eve produces Seth, the spiritual ancestor of those with acquaintance. The rulers manage to cast humanity into a state of ignorance of true spiritual reality, and they harass people with the flood and the temptations of sex and precious metals. The period of human oblivion will come to an end when God's spirit returns to rectify the lack of acquaintance and to facilitate the return to the entirety of the spiritual power dispersed in humanity.

In contrast to the *Secret Book, The Revelation of Adam* attributes loss of acquaintance to the separation of Adam and Eve, and it more firmly ties the survival of the spiritual power to a specific "race" of people. According to this work, when Adam and Eve still exist together as a spiritual androgyne, the female revelatory principle is able to teach Adam "an account of acquaintance with the eternal god" (*Ap. Adam* 64:12-14). The rulers, however, separate the male and the female, and the glory of acquaintance departs from them and enters "the seed belonging to great aeons" (65:3-5). Adam, now lacking acquaintance, then receives a revelation from higher beings, which he shares with his son Seth. This revelation explains how the flood of Genesis 6 and the destruction of Sodom and Gomorrah in Genesis 19 will be failed attempts of the rulers to destroy the "other race" or "Those People," who will descend from Seth and possess the possibility of acquaintance with the entirety. Adam looks forward to the arrival of a savior, "That Human Being," whose appearance will lead to the destruction of the rulers and the human beings whom they have led astray and the salvation of all "Those People" who have acquaintance with the eternal God.

*The Reality of the Rulers* places the rulers' erotic attraction and violent hostility to the female spiritual principle at the center of its version of Genesis. When the eternal beings shine down an image of incorruptibility from above, the rulers become "enamored" with it. They create Adam in order to entice and trap the image, but their human form remains immobile. The spirit from above enters Adam and enables him to move. When the rulers create Eve, the spiritual principle, coded as feminine, passes into her, and the rulers soon become enamored of Eve as well and attempt to rape her. But the spirit escapes from Eve into the tree of life (Genesis 2:9) and eventually into the snake, whose instruction to the human beings to eat from the tree of acquaintance with good evil results in their awareness of their lack of acquaintance. The appearance of a female character named Nōrea, a sister of Seth, brings humanity's gradual improvement in knowledge of spiritual matters. This improvement provokes the rulers to cause the flood and to attempt to rape Nōrea, who finds rescue and receives revelations from the luminary Ēlē-lēth. This work looks forward to the arrival of a savior, "the true human being," who will bring final salvation to Nōrea's offspring and destruction to the rulers.

From these three examples one can see that gender is a prominent theme in the Gnostic myth and, just as in the divine realm, operates in complex and ambiguous ways in the primeval era that the Gnostics imagined.[22] For example, the rulers' erotic attraction to the spiritual principle drives the action in *The Reality of the Rulers*. Curiously, Ialdabaōth and the rulers who lust for a spiritual principle coded female and embodied in women such as Eve and Nōrea are described as both "bestial" and "androgynous," and androgyny denotes origin in the material realm (*Hyp. Arch.* 87:29; 94:18–19). Their attempted rapes demonstrate the violent nature of the desire to possess the image of incorruptibility. Eve and Nōrea both resist the rulers, but the work devalues women in the flesh (the fleshly Eve is raped, while the spiritual one escapes) and instead places worth in a purely spiritual existence.[23] The active, saving work of female characters like Afterthought and Nōrea and the depiction of the divine instructing principle as feminine do not tend to disrupt the superiority of the masculine within the overall Gnostic worldview.

Moreover, these stories present strong connections among violence, aggression, ignorance, and sexual desire. The *Secret Book* explains that sexual intercourse originated in Ialdabaōth's rape of Eve, in whom Ialdabaōth (in one version) "sowed a seed of desire." And thus follow the sexual reproduction of embodied human beings, their reception of the rulers' misleading "counterfeit spirit," and their existence in the "cave" of the material world (*Ap. John* II 24:26–33). Later Ialdabaōth sends his angels to seduce other human women and to introduce them to precious metals and the "great anxieties" that lust for such possessions produces (*Ap. John* II 29:14–30:1). Gnostic readers learned from such accounts the demonic origins of sexual desire, anger, avarice, and other passions, and thus they could begin to resist the rulers, to reform their behaviors, and to acquire the virtues.

To complete the narrative of salvation, most Gnostic writings claim that the final return of the lost power to the entirety and the consequent destruction of the lower universe and its rulers would follow the appearance of a savior (the Forethought of the Entirety, or the Great Seth) in human form. Sometimes this appearance is said to be the third time that the savior has arrived (and scholars debate what the first two advents might be), and it can be portrayed as still to come in the future (when it is predicted by someone like Adam) or to have already taken place. And so in the *Secret Book* Forethought claims that in her third advent she "entered the midst of their [human beings'] prison," that is, "the prison of the body" (*Ap. John* II 31:3–4). After three generations, promises Ēlēlēth in *The Reality of the Rulers*, the Gnostic "posterity" will appear, free from the rulers' bondage. At that time "the true human being, within a modeled form," will come to reveal the spirit of truth and teach the saved posterity about everything (*Hyp. Arch.* 96:27–97:21).

These works do not explicitly claim that Jesus is the embodied incarnation of the savior (although such may be implied by the *Secret Book*, in which Christ is the revealer figure), but other Gnostic books do. In *First Thought in Three Forms,* First Thought describes at length her final appearance in a body, during which she taught human beings about spiritual truths, and concludes: "For my part, I put on Jesus; I extracted him from the accursed wood; and I made him stand at rest in the dwelling places of his parent" (50:12–15). According to *The Holy Book of the Great Invisible Spirit,* it is the Great Seth who "put on" Jesus and thereby brought down the rulers (*Gos. Eg.* IV 75:15–24). These passages suggest that the incarnate savior figure in *The Revelation of Adam,* "That Human Being" who performs signs and wonders and provokes the wrath of the rulers, is also Jesus. After all, Adam prophesies that the rulers "will chastise the flesh of the human being upon whom the holy spirit has come" (*Ap. Adam* 77:1–18).

Modern scholars typically consider a "docetic" understanding of Christ to be an attribute of Gnosticism. Docetism is the idea that Jesus did not have a material human body; he only "seemed" (in Greek, *dokein*) to have flesh and blood. According to this view, Jesus did not really suffer or need to eat, but he did such things to fit in, so to speak, among human beings. The Gnostic works that I just mentioned certainly do not have a high opinion of the body (a "prison"), nor do they consider Jesus' body to be an essential part of the savior, who "puts on" the human Jesus like a garment that he or she can easily remove. These works, however, do not appear to deny the reality of Jesus' body, for the rulers can chastise his flesh. Indeed, the Gnostic work *Melchizedek* condemns Christians who claim that Jesus was not really born or did not really eat, have flesh, and suffer: Jesus did all these things, the author asserts (5:1–17). The Gnostic savior truly did become incarnate.

Like other Christians, Gnostics lived in an in-between time: final salvation and revelation had come in Jesus, but the consummation of the end times that his arrival initiated had not yet come. The rulers were still in charge of this universe, and human beings still needed to be awakened to their true nature and the reality of the spiritual realm. Gnostic literature makes this message of awakening available to readers, although Gnostic witnesses perhaps differ on how many readers are prospective Gnostics. For example, *The Revelation of Adam* seems to suggest that Gnostics form only a small portion of present-day human beings. In biblical antiquity they were limited to the "other" race of "Those People," and at the end of time "the peoples" of the earth acclaim the seed of Seth and lament their own complete destruction: "Indeed, now we know that our souls are going to die with death" (83:8–84:3). In this respect, the *Revelation* echoes the views of early Christians like Paul, who imagined salvation only for the relatively small number of God's elect and the damnation of all others.

On the other hand, *The Secret Book According to John* contains an extensive discussion of human salvation. It envisions a conflict within and among human beings between the spirit of life, which originates in the entirety, and the counterfeit spirit, which the rulers create to lead human beings astray. Human beings who fall victim to the counterfeit spirit do not die forever, but their souls reincarnate, perhaps multiple times, until they attain acquaintance and salvation. Only apostates, "those who have gained acquaintance and then turned away," appear destined for eternal punishment (*Ap. John* II 25:16–27:31). This view resembles that of the third-century Christian theologian Origen, who believed that over countless ages of time God would eventually lead all fallen souls back to himself, perhaps even the soul of Satan.

The Gnostic myth, then, is a story of return. An original state of fullness, harmony, and acquaintance in the entirety falls into lack, discord, and ignorance, and yet the original state of perfection will be achieved once again, thanks to the work of the immortal beings. That which the entirety lost will be recovered. So, too, Adam and Eve once enjoyed acquaintance with the ultimate God, the gift of the power that Ialdabaōth unwittingly passed on to them, but their descendants have fallen into ignorance and oblivion, having forgotten their true origin and having mistaken Ialdabaōth and his rulers for genuine divinities. And yet this lack among human beings will be filled as well, for the story of Genesis is the story of how the Barbēlō aeon and others preserve the spirit of life among human beings, despite the rulers' continued efforts to seize it and destroy human beings. The first step in achieving moral reformation and religious insight is a correct diagnosis of the human situation. The Gnostic myth takes seriously the ills of this life—the passions that hinder our virtue, the material body that obstructs our knowledge, and the fate that constricts our choices—but it is ultimately a message of hope, of reformation and salvation through Jesus, the incarnate savior.

## The Gnostics and Other Christians

Although surviving Gnostic literature is primarily pseudepigraphic mythology, allowing little room for overt references to contemporary persons or events, it does exhibit several strategies by which the Gnostics differentiated themselves from other groups that also drew on the biblical tradition. Because Gnostics differed from their competitors precisely on how to appropriate the biblical narrative in the wake of the Jesus event, most of these strategies revolved around the interpretation of the Bible. The Gnostics claimed authority for their readings primarily by appealing to sources of special divine revelation. In the *Secret Book*, "the savior" Christ reveals the existence of the higher entirety and the true meaning of Genesis to the disciple John "mystically" in a post-ascension appearance (II 32:2). More typical is a revelation told by a character in the biblical narrative—Adam *(Ap. Adam)*, Seth *(Gos. Eg.)*, or the exclusively Gnostic character Nōrea *(Hyp. Arch.)*; after the manner of other Jewish apocalypses of this period, the revelation is purported to have been written down and preserved secretly until the present crucial eschatological moment. In writings such as these, no contemporary Gnostic teacher claims his or her own interpretive authority or superior education in biblical exegesis: readings are true because a divine being or divinely inspired person from the past spoke them. An apparent exception to this pattern is *The Reality of the Rulers,* in which an anonymous teacher addresses an equally nameless student in the first person, but even this author appeals to the authority of "the great apostle," Paul, who was "inspired by the spirit of the parent of truth" (*Hyp. Arch.* 86:20–27), and later produces verbatim a lengthy revelation of Nōrea (starting at 93:13). His retelling of the early chapters of Genesis mimics the style and diction of the Septuagint, so that the reader can hardly tell the difference between the original text and its revision. The Gnostics, then, presented their interpretations of the Bible as not in fact their interpretations, but as revelations given by Adam, Seth, Paul, or Christ himself.

Despite this pseudepigraphic mode of exposition, Gnostic authors at times reveal their competition with other readers in their milieu. In the *Secret Book* the savior tells John that what happened "is not as you have heard that Moses wrote" (*Ap. John* II 22:22–23; cf. 13:19–21; 29:6–7). In this way the author implicitly admits that other people read Genesis differently and even that there is a generally accepted reading (that is, "literal" meaning) that he expects his reader to know. The author can also offer brief arguments for his exegetical views (e.g., II 13:9–13). Irenaeus reports that some Gnostics defended their exegetical methods by claiming that different voices speak in the biblical text—the different demonic rulers, Ialdabaōth, Wisdom—and that the careful reader must distinguish among them.[24] More significantly, some Gnostic authors found in biblical characters or groups representatives or prototypes of contemporary persons, most obviously themselves.[25] Thus, *The Revelation of Adam* appears to identify the posterity of Noah's son Shem as the Jews, while the descendants of Ham and Japhtheth represent Gentiles (*Ap. Adam* 73:1–29). The prototypes of the Gnostics include "some other race," "Those People," who turn out to be the residents of Sodom and Gomorrah whom "God Almighty" attempts to destroy (75:9–76:7), and 400,000 people who leave the posterities of Ham and Japhtheth to "sojourn with Those People" (73:13–24). The 400,000 may represent converts to the Gnostic sect. In the *Secret Book* "the immovable race" is saved from the flood, but not in an ark, a symbol of the Church in some Christian exegesis (*Ap. John* II 28:32–29:15). As they made the Genesis narrative their own myth of origins, the Gnostics found ways to use the biblical narrative to legitimate themselves and to delegitimate others.

In so doing, the Gnostics used the language of race and kinship to delineate themselves and other groups. As we have seen, the proper name of the sect was the "Gnostic school of thought" *(gnōstikē haire-sis)*, a self-promotional designation that identified it as that school of thought capable of supplying "knowledge" *(gnōsis)*.[26] We know of other groups who called themselves a *hairesis* ("school of thought"): adher-ents of the medical school of thought associated with Herophilus called themselves "the *hairesis* of Herophilus," and the Jewish author Josephus proclaimed that he followed "the *hairesis* of the Pharisees."[27] But the Gnostics' terms for themselves as the ideal religious people were racial or ethnic: "the immovable race," "the seed of Seth," "Those People." On one level, this language reflects the Genesis narratives that the Gnostics used as the basis for their mythological works. Genesis tells stories of genealogical descent and of conflict between good and bad siblings (like Cain and Abel), and thus readers from antiquity to today have used these stories as maps for thinking about the interactions of the saved and their opponents throughout history. Augustine of Hippo, for example, used the stories of Genesis as the basis for *The City of God*, his own tale of two cities, that of God and that of this world. The Gnostics stand in this tradition, with *The Revelation of Adam*, as we have seen, taking this mode of interpretation to the greatest detail among Gnostic works.

More generally, the Gnostic vocabulary of race reflects the wider an-cient practice of using ethnic or kinship language for groups that shared the same religious practices and seeing religious practice as part of the definition of a nation or kinship group.[28] Ancient people lived in a world full of gods, which they associated with different ethnic groups; differ-ent peoples had different traditions of worshiping their own god or gods. The Jews were no different: they worshiped specifically the God of Israel. As Paula Fredriksen has put it, in antiquity "gods run in the blood," and "cult is an ethnic designation," while in turn "ethnicity is a cultic designation."[29] And so the language of ethnicity, race, and kinship came naturally to people when they spoke of their religious communi-ties. Christians other than the Gnostics frequently claimed that they represented a "new race."[30]

Opponents of the Gnostics such as Clement of Alexandria and Ori-gen, however, charged that the Gnostics and the Valentinians used such language literally.[31] They argued that the Gnostics considered religious identities to be predetermined and fixed: Gnostics, as the offspring or seed of Seth, were saved "by nature"; all other people, destined for destruc-tion "by nature." Salvation or damnation was genetically determined, we would say. So the fourth-century heresiologist Epiphanius describes the teachings of "the Sethians," whose myth seems to be the Gnostic myth.[32] Many modern scholars have accepted this interpretation. But in general the use of ethnic or kinship language to speak of religious identity in antiquity did not necessarily imply such deterministic beliefs: ancient people could imagine persons moving from one "nation" to another.[33] People could turn away from their ancestral gods to the god of another people and even become part of their new ethnicity. As we have seen, several Gnostic texts appear to assume that people can choose to become a Gnostic and to apostatize after they have joined the sect.[34] *The Revelation of Adam* appears to take a highly literal approach to genealogical descent in the Bible: the descendants of Noah's son Shem represent Jews; those of Ham and Japhtheth, the Gentiles; while the primeval Gnostics form their own ethnic group, "Those People," "the undominated race." And yet even here the prospect of conversion appears in the 400,000 people who leave the descendants of Ham and Japhtheth and "enter some other land and sojourn with Those People who came into being out of great eternal acquaintance . . . The shadow of their [Those People's] power will guard those who have sojourned with them for all evil deeds and all foul desires" (*Ap. Adam* 73:13–24). The 400,000 are made descendants of Seth, members of the undominated race, by adoption, which was regularly practiced in antiquity and served as a common metaphor for conversion.[35]

*The Gospel of Judas* stands out from the other surviving Gnostic works because its narrative takes place not in the primordial era of Adam, Eve, and Noah, but during the ministry of Jesus, and it explicitly condemns rival Christian groups as vehemently as Irenaeus or any other heresiologist. Although the disciple Judas is far from perfect and appears destined to play a negative, if essential, role in the drama of salvation, he alone among the disciples knows Jesus' true origin in the Barbēlō and receives from Jesus a revelation of the true facts concerning God, creation, and the future. The other disciples ignorantly celebrate the Eucharist in honor of their false god, and Jesus accuses them of leading numerous people astray, bringing them not to *gnōsis* and life, but to ignorance and death. They are priests sacrificing human beings on the altar of their own immorality and lack of knowledge. In this case, the Gnostic author is explicit about his views of other Christians: they are wrong.

Gnostic authors, then, were aware of other believers in Jesus whose views differed from theirs. In response, they presented their ideas as correct interpretations of the Jewish Scriptures, which divine and authoritative figures had revealed to them. The Gnostics identified themselves with Seth, the third son of Adam and Eve, and used the narratives of Genesis to identify themselves as the unique possessors of the true *gnōsis* of God. They were the seed of Seth and the immovable race.

## Ritual: Baptism and Mystical Ascent

A person did not have to be born to other descendants of Seth to become one of the chosen ones. Rather, one of the most distinctive features of the sect appears to have been its ritual of baptism, which incorporated one into the seed of Seth or immovable race and facilitated ascent to contemplation of the divine.[36] According to *The Revelation of Adam*, the "seed" that will be saved consists of those who "will have received his name"—that is, Seth's name—"upon the water" (83:5–6). Two Gnostic writings (*First Thought in Three Forms* and *The Holy Book of the Great Invisible Spirit*) contain fairly extensive, albeit highly stylized and symbolic, depictions of this ritual, and others refer to some of its distinctive elements and presiding divinities or remark on its centrality to salvation.[37] In *The Secret Book According to John*, for example, Forethought describes how she has saved human beings who were in "the prison of the body," unaware of their divine origin and destiny. She calls a person out of "heavy sleep," encourages him or her to "follow your root, which is myself, the compassionate," and warns against the machinations of the demonic rulers. "And," she proclaims at the climax, "I raised and sealed that person, with the light of the water of five seals, so that from thenceforth death might not have power over that person" (*Ap. John* 31:3–25). The "water of five seals" refers to the distinctively Gnostic form of baptism, which one recognizes by its "five seals."

What happened at this baptism? Oblique, symbolic references in *First Thought in Three Forms* suggest a series of ritual actions, which we can tell from other sources were followed by a hymnic response (48:1–49:6). In this work, First Thought—that is, the Barbēlō—says that first she has "stripped off" from the candidate chaos, darkness, and other elements of this world; the person is subsequently "clothed in shining light" and "dressed in a robe belonging to the robes of light." Likewise, *The Holy Book of the Great Invisible Spirit* refers to the "armor of loveliness and light" that the baptized person dons (*Gos. Eg.* IV 79:14–16). As in other forms of Christian baptism, the removal of clothing required for washing in water symbolizes the removal of an old state of existence, and special new clothing represents a transformed state. As *First Thought in Three Forms* presents the ritual, it seems that the person is "washed in the wellspring of the water of life" after putting on the ritual robe. Both of these steps, stripping/clothing and washing, take place under the direction of divine beings who are called "enrobers" and "baptists," respectively. Additional steps follow, which also have presiding divinities, but their actual forms are less easy to discern. The baptized person is given "a throne from the throne of glory" by "the enthroners," and then "the glorifiers" glorify the candidate "with the glory of the kinship." Finally, "those who catch up" take the person "into the luminous places of that person's kinship"—a reference perhaps to some form of mystical ascent and contemplation.[38] This description ends with a reference to "the five seals," which come from "the light of the mother, First Thought," the Barbēlō.

Although the five seals are the most distinctive feature of Gnostic baptism, scholars do not know what they were, but there are some plausible ideas.[39] In *First Thought in Three Forms,* there are five steps in baptism that also have sets of presiding divinities—enrobing, washing, enthroning, glorifying, and catching up to luminous places—and so it is possible that these steps are the five seals. Alternatively, when Forethought in the *Secret Book* refers to "the water of the five seals," perhaps she refers to five baptisms in the water (that is, five separate immersions or washings). Non-Gnostic Christian works also speak of "sealing" in connection with baptism, most often referring to anointing with oil. Oil placed on a person, sometimes in the shape of the cross, marked the baptized as belonging to Christ and sealed him or her against malevolent powers. Five seals might, then, refer to five instances of anointing, perhaps corresponding to the five baptismal steps that appear in *First Thought,* or to the five senses and their associated body parts (eyes, ears, hands, mouth, nose), or to the five organs that corresponded to faculties of the soul (two eyes, two ears, mouth). On the other hand, there are few explicit references to the anointing of human beings in Gnostic works. The author of *The Reality of the Rulers* does say that the final savior, "the true human being, within a modeled form," will "anoint" the saved people "with the ointment of eternal life" (*Hyp. Arch.* 96:33–97:4), and the visionary Gnostic in *Zōstrianos* reports being anointed during his mystical ascent (63:22). Of course, the anointed one (Christ) is a significant figure in the divine realm. But otherwise, anointing of human beings is not a prominent theme. In the end, the precise nature of the baptismal five seals remains a mystery.

Whatever the five seals were in practice, in *The Holy Book of the Great Invisible Spirit*, "the five seals" refers also to divine beings in the eternal realm (IV 66:25–26), although it is not clear which ones. In fact, the *Holy Book* recounts the Gnostic myth in a way that is useful to communal worship, as a prelude to an actual baptismal ceremony. Modern Christians in liturgically oriented churches may compare it with an Easter Vigil and its series of biblical readings that tell the history of salvation, interrupted by Psalms and canticles, and which culminate in baptism. In addition to incorporating the five seals into the spiritual fullness, the narrator in the *Holy Book* pauses several times in his narration of divine emanations to allow the incorruptible beings to give praise to those that are higher than they, and thus the work is filled with short hymns of praise and growing lists of divine beings worthy of glory. Those hearing the *Holy Book* being read could have joined in these hymns of praise. The *Holy Book*'s history of salvation culminates in the Great Seth's incarnation in Jesus, through whom he "established the holy and the baptism that is higher than the heavens" (IV 75:10–17). The work concludes with a lengthy hymn in praise of Jesus and expressing gratitude for the benefits of baptism: "For this reason, the fragrance of life is within me: For it has been mixed with water to serve as a prototype for all the rulers" (III 67:22–24). The Gnostic myth may strike the modern reader as a complex and highly intellectual approach to God, but the *Holy Book* closely connects the myth to a ritual that bestows salvation and communicates a religious disposition of heartfelt praise and gratitude.

Although it involved water, was instituted through Jesus as the Great Seth's incarnation, and promised that its recipients "shall not taste death," Gnostic baptism appears to have shared few features with the versions of baptism that one finds in other early Christian sources. For example, there are no references to baptism "in the name of the Lord Jesus," as in the Acts of the Apostles (e.g., Acts 8:16) or "in the name of the Father and of the Son and of the Holy Spirit," as in the Gospel of Matthew (28:19) and the *Didache* (7:1–3), a church manual from around 100 CE. The central characteristic of Gnostic baptism was the mysterious five seals, and it took place under the guidance of a distinctively Gnostic cast of divine beings, led by Mikheus, Mikhar, and Mnēsinous. The Gnostics contrasted their water baptism with those of competing groups: others, they said, have "defiled the water of life" (*Ap. Adam* 84:17–18). They did not present their rite as a more advanced or more mystical version of a more generally available baptism. It was their peculiarly distinctive rite and must have had its own developmental history.

Likewise, Gnostics appear to have differed from other Christians by not observing a Eucharist or any other ritual meal that commemorated the death of Christ. After all, it was not primarily through his death that Jesus saved human beings, but by incarnating the savior (whether Forethought or the great Seth), awakening people to their true divine identity, and bringing the means of acquaintance with God. In fact, the Gnostic author of *The Gospel of Judas* severely criticizes the Eucharist as a ceremony that offers praise to Ialdabaōth, the god of this world. The sacrificial victim that other Christian leaders offer on their altars is not bread or the body of Christ, but the people that they lead astray into ignorance and death (39:18–40:1). "Stop sacrificing animals!" Jesus commands his wayward disciples, referring to the animals that symbolize their deceived Christian followers (41:1–2). Instead, the *Holy Book* associates baptism with the crucifixion of Jesus (as, of course, Christians like Paul did as well). According to this work, the great Seth established baptism "by the living reason-born Jesus, whom the great Seth put on (like a garment). And he nailed down the powers of the thirteen aeons and made them inactive; at his instigation they are fetched and they are removed" (*Gos. Eg.* IV 75:11–21). The phrase "nailed down" suggests that the crucifixion was the means by which the great Seth, incarnate in Jesus, defeated the lower powers.

Baptism, then, seems to have been the Gnostics' central and defining ritual, and it is possible that a Gnostic may have experienced baptism not simply a single time as an initiation into the group, but multiple times as a means to increasingly higher knowledge of God. The composition of *The Holy Book of the Great Invisible Spirit* as a mythic narration leading to baptism may suggest that baptism was a repeated ceremony, but even more intriguing is the Gnostic work *Zōstrianos*. This book tells the story of an ancient figure named Zōstrianos, who experiences a mystical journey through ascending aeons of the entirety until he reaches the Barbēlō aeon and attempts to contemplate the Invisible Spirit. As he reaches higher levels of abstraction and knowledge, Zōstrianos undergoes repeated baptisms, in which he is washed with the waters that belong to each aeon. In fact, he is baptized five times into the self-originate aeon alone. After the fifth baptism, he "became divine" (*Zōs.* 53:15–19).

Remarks such as a reference to Mikheus and Mikhar as "the powers that preside over living waters" (6:9–10) indicate that Zōstrianos is experiencing the same Gnostic baptism that we find in *First Thought in Three Forms* and *The Holy Book of the Great Invisible Spirit*. Some interpreters conclude, then, that a Gnostic would have been baptized multiple times, perhaps facilitating or commemorating advances in his or her knowledge of Gnostic teachings and contemplative insight. Other readers, however, cite Zōstrianos's multiple baptisms in spiritual aeons as evidence that baptism for the Gnostics was primarily if not exclusively a metaphor for the acquisition of acquaintance with God and other divine beings. And indeed, *The Revelation of Adam* explicitly identifies acquaintance *(gnōsis)* with baptism: the author says that the content of his book "is the secret acquaintance of Adam that he delivered to Seth and which, for those who are acquainted with eternal acquaintance through the agency of the reason-born beings and the incorruptible luminaries who emanated from the holy seed, is holy baptism" (*Ap. Adam* 85:22–29). In this view, the Gnostics may not have observed a physical ritual of baptism at all, but instead promoted the *gnōsis* that they offered as the mystical equivalent of baptism.

I am inclined to think, however, that the Gnostics did in fact practice their ritual of baptism. For example, the *Holy Book* makes the most sense as a work that would have been ritually performed, and the criticism of other believers who have defiled baptismal waters suggest that the Gnostics quarreled with others over actual ritual activity involving water. Still, the meaning and value of baptism for them must have lay in the mystical acquaintance with God that it bestowed. The authors of the Letters to the Ephesians and the Colossians in the New Testament could speak of the baptism that Pauline Christians practiced in grand, cosmological terms, suggesting, for example, that it raised Christians to sit with Christ "in the heavenly places" (Ephesians 2:6). So, too, *Zōstrianos* portrays Gnostic baptism as both the means to and the metaphor for mystical ascent to contemplation of the aeons.

The Gnostics believed that the human intellect could experience *gnōsis*, that is, acquaintance with God, within this mortal life, however fleetingly. They portrayed this experience primarily as an ascent to higher knowledge that was both intellectual and cosmic.[40] Intellectually, the Gnostic could ascend by contemplating increasingly abstract levels of existence, starting by understanding one's own existence and that of other lower divine beings, advancing to the contemplation of higher aeons, ultimately the Barbēlō, and attempting to gain some imperfect acquaintance with the ineffable first principle, the Invisible Spirit. This form of ascent can be traced back to Plato's *Symposium,* which encourages the educated man to ascend to contemplation of Beauty itself by loving and understanding increasingly more abstract objects of desire (from the body of a single beautiful boy, to the beautiful body per se, to the beautiful soul, to the principles that govern the soul, and so on to Beauty itself). Because Plato believed that erotic desire and intellectual knowledge go together, a man's desire for a beautiful body can be transformed into love for a beautiful soul and then into intellectual enjoyment of ideas. Plato presented the final vision of Beauty itself as coming to the contemplative person gratuitously—"all of a sudden"—and yet after a long period of intellectual effort.[41]

Cosmically, Gnostic texts portray the intellects of human heroes (Zōstrianos, Marsanes, and "Foreigner" in works named for them) as leaving their bodies and journeying upward through the heavenly realms, guided and instructed by angels or other heavenly beings. Here the Gnostics are indebted to Jewish apocalypses such as *2 Enoch* that similarly describe pious figures being guided through heavenly realms by one or more angels and eventually gaining a vision of God himself. In the case of *2 Enoch* the hero's righteousness in following the Jewish Law and remaining faithful to the God of Israel qualifies him for his special ascent and tour of the heavens, and he returns from his experience to exhort others to righteous living and fidelity to God. The combination of these two traditions—Platonism's intellectual ascent through increasing abstraction and apocalyptic Judaism's cosmic ascent through heavenly realms—is a distinctive feature of Gnostic mysticism. (A Platonist example of a heavenly journey may be seen in Cicero's description of Scipio's dream.)[42] Gnostic authors assert both that the human intellect has the capacity to understand increasingly abstract levels of being and ultimately God and that divine revelation and guidance is necessary for such human contact with the ultimate principle.

In *Zōstrianos,* then, the hero engages in a process of study and contemplation that requires his own effort and mental concentration, and he follows a series of angels and other divine beings who guide him upward into the heavenly realms. As Zōstrianos himself tells the story, "by means of intellect" he was able to turn himself away from material things and toward spiritual realities, and he engaged in a program of asceticism, philosophical study, and teaching (1:10–27). Such a program is both necessary and insufficient for acquaintance with God: it helps Zōstrianos to see the "pettiness" of ordinary embodied existence and to formulate questions about higher reality, but it leaves him "anguished and depressed," still seeking the "realm of repose" beyond "the perceptible world" (2:24–3:28). At this point the "the angel of acquaintance" appears to Zōstrianos and invites him to pass through the lower realms and ascend to the entirety. The hero abandons his physical body, boards a luminous cloud, and undertakes a complex upward journey in which he meets several divine revealers, undergoes repeated baptisms, and gains knowledge of increasingly abstract levels of reality, up to the Barbēlō. At the apex of his journey Zōstrianos seeks to understand the Invisible Spirit itself, but this act is described as "reckless" (128:19–129:1), not so dissimilar from Wisdom's original failed attempt to think on her own. The act may be "reckless" because ultimate acquaintance with the Invisible Spirit must come, as in Platonic mysticism, not by human initiative, but "all of a sudden," as a gift. In any event, Zōstrianos then descends and returns to his physical body. Like the Jewish hero Enoch, Zōstrianos then preaches the message of moral reformation and acquaintance to other people (130:13–132:5). In this account, Zōstrianos gains mystical contact with the divine through his own ascetic and intellectual efforts and through revelation from divine beings, but falls short of ultimate *gnōsis* with the highest God.

The roles of divine guidance and revelation and human effort and capacity are not at odds in Gnostic mysticism because the human intellect possesses the same structure as that of the divine entirety. The human mind is a kind of miniature representation of the aeons that emanate from the ultimate God, as in fact we share in the spiritual essence that somehow passed from the entirety through Ialdabaōth to us. For this reason, the Gnostic could also contemplate God by contemplating his or her own intellect, as does the hero of *The Foreigner*.[43] The Foreigner, literally, "One of Another Kind," is a mythical human being, perhaps even the ancient human Seth, whom the Bible identifies as "another seed," that is, not of the same kind as Abel (Genesis 5:3). In the fourth century, Epiphanius claimed to know Christians ("Archontics") who called Seth "the Foreigner."[44] In any event, our Foreigner writes to his disciple Messos (perhaps a pun meaning "Middle Man" or "Intermediary") and describes his own mystical ascent to the Barbēlō aeon and the series of revelatory discourses that he received from the eternal being Iouēl. Unlike Zōstrianos, the Foreigner does not experience baptisms in the aeons that he visits, and the revelations that he receives concern only the highest aeons, particularly the Barbēlō. When the Foreigner reaches the highest aspect of reality below the Invisible Spirit, Iouēl concludes his discourses with a promise that the Foreigner will receive a revelation of the Unknowable One after a period of one hundred years (56:21–27).

Rather than being discouraged by this news, the Foreigner spends the next century preparing himself through interior deliberation, and his work is rewarded when he is taken up out of his body to "a holy place," where he can see the eternal beings and aeons of which Iouēl had spoken one hundred years earlier (57:27–58:38). Now eternal beings instruct the Foreigner to practice a form of mystical ascent that must have been more realistic than a heavenly journey for an actual Gnostic of the second or third century. The Foreigner learns that he must turn within himself and contemplate sequentially the structures of his own mind through increasingly abstract stages of interior "withdrawal" (59:10–60:12). An allusion to such a practice occurs in Zōstrianos, which states that the saved person can "withdraw inward. For such a person becomes god and has withdrawn into god" (44:20–22). Zeke Masur has called this mental withdrawal an "act of contemplative self-reversion"; human beings can perform it because some stamp or remnant of the Invisible Spirit's initial act of self-knowledge, which resulted in the emanation of the entirety, persists in the human intellect.[45] As he performs this self-contemplation, the Foreigner gains acquaintance with aspects of the Barbēlō aeon (blessedness, vitality, and reality) by understanding himself—"as I really am!" He discovers the Barbēlō as "that which existed within me" (60:13–61:8). He then receives a vision of the Invisible Spirit—in a sudden, gratuitous way, as in Plato's Symposium—but his desire to understand or to grasp the ultimate God is met with a speech that describes at length the unknowable nature of that God (61:8–67:37). Ultimately, the Foreigner learns that he paradoxically understands the Invisible Spirit by not comprehending it. As an eternal being tells him, "Do not [attempt to] comprehend it: for this is impossible. Rather if, through a luminous thought, you should happen to understand it, be uncomprehending of it" (60:8–10). Ultimately, the Foreigner ascends to acquaintance by journeying through his own intellect, and he receives gnōsis of the ultimate God as a gift.

The account of Marsanes' ascent in the work of the same name is highly fragmentary. Like Zōstrianos and the Foreigner, Marsanes ascends through such aeons as the Barbēlō to a nondiscursive vision of the ultimate divinity. Having experienced *gnōsis*, Marsanes now shares what he has learned with other advanced Gnostics: "For it is I who have [contemplated] that which truly exists . . . I have not ceased speaking [of] the Self-Originate, [lest anyone] be [ignorant] in turn of the entire place" (*Mar.* 4:24–26; 5:26–6:1). References to "seals," "washing," and "cleansing" suggest here, too, that baptism facilitates ascent, but *Marsanes* goes beyond baptism to suggest that astrology and the study and pronunciation of alphabetic signs prepares the person for contemplation and ascent (21:14–39:24). The work may refer also to the ritual use of wax and jeweled images (35:1–3). Here the Gnostics incorporated into their spirituality theurgy, that is, ritual practices designed to facilitate the ascent of the human soul to contemplation of the divine or to provoke the descent of higher beings to be present to human beings. Theurgy became popular among Neoplatonist intellectuals in the late third and fourth centuries. In Gnostic use, these practices may have facilitated contemplation by enhancing knowledge of cosmic structures and by granting the ability to manipulate the cosmic rulers.

It is unlikely that any second- or third-century Gnostic anticipated journeying through the heavenly realms to the entirety, guided by eternal beings, but the accounts of Zōstrianos, Marsanes, and the Foreigner would have aided the Gnostic's own mystical reception of *gnōsis* in several ways. First, the Gnostic could gain advanced theoretical knowledge of the entirety's aeons, including the Barbēlō, through the detailed revelations that the mythic heroes receive from their angelic guides and the heroes' own descriptions of what they saw. That these heroes received the information that they share through heavenly ascents and divine revelations would have supported the truth of their religious claims. Second, the writings commend basic practices that could prepare an individual for higher mystical experiences and acquaintance, including philosophical study and asceticism, and *Marsanes* encourages theurgic practices for more advanced Gnostics. Finally, *Zōstrianos* and *Marsanes* suggest that Gnostic baptism was a means to knowledge of God, and *The Foreigner* describes a method of interior withdrawal and contemplation that can grant acquaintance and even lead to an vision of (if not comprehension of) the Invisible Spirit. If the works that narrated the Gnostic myth explained how human knowledge of the divine was lost and yet remained possible for human beings despite demonic opposition, *Zōstrianos*, *Marsanes*, and *The Foreigner* described how the Gnostic could experience knowledge of the divine in the here and now.

Gnostic mysticism left a legacy that extended far beyond the Gnostic school of thought. According to Porphyry, *Zōstrianos* and *The Foreigner* were among the works known to the great philosopher Plotinus and his students. Plotinus devoted many of his seminar meetings to disproving the ideas of these works, and one of his students, Amelius, composed a (now lost) forty-chapter refutation of *Zōstrianos*.[46] The ongoing research of Zeke Mazur suggests not only that Plotinus rejected Gnostic ideas, but also that much of Plotinus's own account of how one achieves mystic union with the One is indebted to Gnostic teachings about mystical ascent.[47] Plotinus's work in turn influenced numerous later Christian mystics, including Augustine and Pseudo-Dionysius.

## The Origins and Character of the Gnostic School of Thought

Having examined Gnostic myth and ritual, albeit briefly, we can consider more sociological questions that interest modern scholars, such as how the Gnostic sect originated. Every ancient observer of the Gnostics (including the non-Christian Porphyry) identifies them as Christians, and nearly all of their surviving writings contain distinctively Christian symbols or references, such as Christ, Jesus, and the apostle Paul. Irenaeus and his fellow Christian heresiologists claimed that the Gnostic sect originated as a false offshoot from true Christianity, but, as we shall see, this claim itself functioned as a powerful strategy of self-differentiation, and few modern scholars believe that there ever was a single true form of Christianity, from which other forms, like the Gnostics, deviated. In the twentieth century some historians of religion argued that an ancient myth about a Primal Man and a divine redeemer originated in eastern regions such as India and then traveled west into the Mediterranean basin through Persia. This original Gnostic myth was neither Jewish nor Christian, but when Jewish, Christian, and pagan intellectuals encountered it, they adapted it to their own traditions. Scholars eventually abandoned this hypothesis for two reasons. First, they grew dissatisfied with understanding a religion or a myth by tracing its motifs back to their alleged origins: religious people borrow from other traditions all the time, and this borrowing in and of itself does not explain why and from where new religious movements arise. Second, many of the sources that historians used to reconstruct the ancient Gnostic "redeemer myth" turned out to be later than the Gnostic texts themselves, sometimes several centuries later.[48]

Instead, many scholars today believe that the Gnostic myth arose among disaffected, philosophically inclined Jews even before they learned about Jesus or Christianity; subsequently, Gnostics added Christian elements like Jesus to their beliefs.[49] It is important to be precise about what this hypothesis of a Jewish origin for "Gnosticism" claims. Certainly all of the earliest Christian groups originated among Jews: Jesus was a Jew, as were all his disciples, and the proclamation of a messiah and son of the God of Israel would make sense first of all only among Jews. Even the mission to the Gentiles was the work of Jews like Paul. But this is not what the hypothesis of the Gnostic sect's Jewish origin means. Rather, the proponents of this theory argue that Jews created the basic Gnostic myth before they had heard of Jesus (even if they may have done so after Jesus' death and the birth of faith in him). The Gnostic myth, according to this view, was a development among Jews independent of any proclamation of Jesus as the savior. Gnostics added references to Jesus to the myth as they became aware of and interacted with Christians.

As evidence for the Jewish origin of the Gnostic sect, scholars point to Gnostic literature's intense interest in Genesis and a few other books of the Septuagint and comparatively little use of the emerging New Testament. Many of the Gnostics' interpretations of Genesis find parallels in Philo and later rabbinic literature, and Gnostic works do not talk much about Jesus, who is subordinated to Seth. Jesus, it is argued, appears to be tacked on as the savior. As we have seen, he is not always explicitly identified as the human being who embodies the savior, and he is variously seen as the incarnation of Forethought/First Thought or the great Seth. Scholars argue, too, that certain Gnostic writings were originally not at all Christian, but then Christianized later. For example, most of *The Secret Book According to John* has no mention of specifically Christian figures and concepts; instead, Christ, the disciple John, and other elements from the Christian Gospels appear only in a brief frame story at the beginning and the end of the book. It is suggested that the Christian frame story was added to an originally non-Christian work. Scholars also claim that *The Revelation of Adam* has no Christian features at all. According to this view, the original Gnostics were Jews who turned against key elements of their tradition, and subsequently the Gnostic school of thought became increasingly Christian.

Why would ancient Jews have decided that the God of Israel, the God of their Bible, was actually the evil and ignorant Ialdabaōth and that

Moses was a flawed and confused author? Scholars have suggested that some Jews may have become disillusioned with the promises of God after Jews suffered defeats by the Romans in the wars of 66–70 and 132–135 CE. After the second of these wars, the Romans expelled the Jews from the holy city of Jerusalem, which they reorganized as a pagan city called Aelia Capitolina.[50] Alternatively, perhaps some Jews wanted to distance themselves from Jewish tradition after Jews in Alexandria and other cities rose up in defense of their rights and were brutally crushed in 115–117.[51] All of these experiences may have caused thoughtful Jews to experience a "crisis of history."[52] Was it still possible to trust in the God of the Bible? Jewish intellectuals may also have become increasingly embarrassed by the God of Genesis, who walks around in an earthly garden and displays such human characteristics as ignorance ("Adam, where are you?"), anger, and regret. Platonist philosophy convinced them that a truly perfect God would be remote, entirely spiritual, and beyond all emotions—hence, the Invisible Spirit, who exists beyond the realm of the imperfect creator Ialdabaōth.[53]

The hypothesis that the Gnostic school of thought originated in Judaism apart from Christianity has some attractive features. It accounts for the ambivalent authority that Gnostics granted to the Septuagint, and it avoids Irenaeus's model of heretical deviance (at least from Christianity). But it is not convincing for several reasons. First, many of the parallels to Gnostic exegesis in Jewish literature come from writings that must be dated to centuries after the Gnostics. Second, it is not certain that writings such as the *Secret Book* did pass through a literary history of Christianization,[54] and we have seen that even *The Revelation of Adam* appears to refer, albeit obliquely, to the sufferings of Jesus (77:4–18). The argument that certain Gnostic literary works lack "Christian" features and do not dwell on Jesus enough presupposes a certain view of what is genuinely Christian or how early Christians ought to write and measures Gnostic literature against that presupposition. One thinks of the Letter of James in the New Testament, which similarly displays few "Christian" characteristics. Instead, like James, Gnostic writings demonstrate that Christians expressed their beliefs in diverse ways. Plus, works like the *Secret Book* and *The Revelation of Adam* seek to retell the stories of Genesis, and so their authors may have purposefully avoided explicit references to Jesus. *The Gospel of Judas* is undeniably Christian and, along with the *Secret Book,* is one of the earliest datable Gnostic works. Its long revelation from Jesus to Judas, dealing with creation and the primeval period, similarly lacks distinctively Christian characters.

There are no signs in Gnostic literature that its authors were disillusioned with the God of Israel due to political catastrophes,[55] and the example of Philo shows that commitment to Platonism and a Platonic view of God need not lead to considering the God of Genesis demonic. One must ask whether it is plausible to imagine Jews deciding that the God of the Bible is wicked, not merely subordinate to a higher principle, solely out of disillusionment of any kind. *The Fourth Book of Ezra,* an originally Jewish work of around 100 CE, wrestles with the problem of God's justice in the wake of the political misfortunes of the Jews: Ezra complains bitterly, but the work asserts God's judgment and love for Israel, as inscrutable as his ways of showing these may be. It seems more likely that reconceiving the God of Israel as the wicked and foolish Ialdabaōth required also the proclamation of some new insight that called into question the value of the Torah while also drawing from it, as can be seen in, say, the letters of Paul or the Fourth Gospel. Finally, the clear distinction between Judaism and Christianity assumed by much current scholarly discussion probably did not exist in the early decades of the second century; rather, this was one of the distinctions that authors such as Justin Martyr were seeking to create.[56] The Gnostics may in fact exemplify the nonexistence of the categories "Judaism" and "Christianity." For them Jesus made a difference, but not the same kind of difference as he did for other Christians.

When I and other scholars argue that the Gnostic school of thought originated as a Christian movement, we are not endorsing Irenaeus's model of early Christian history. That is, we do not believe that Gnostics deviated from an originally singular and uniform Christianity, introducing innovations into the message of the original followers of Jesus. Instead, we imagine that the ministry, death, and resurrection appearances of Jesus fostered a variety of religious responses, which developed and interacted with each other in diverse ways. One of the responses to which Jesus gave rise was the Gnostic school of thought.

Historians debate as well what kind of group the Gnostics may have formed. Was their community a tight-knit band of committed believers, or a loose association of mystics, or what? Very few scholars dispute that the literary works that I have assigned to the Gnostic school of thought form some sort of literary tradition (which they have usually called "Sethianism"), but the writings give us very little social information about the people who might lie behind them. Irenaeus calls the group a "school of thought," which may indicate merely a shared intellectual tradition, and he and other ancient authors give the names of prominent Valentinian teachers, but do not do so for the Gnostics.[57] Porphyry does supply some names of persons who might be Gnostics.[58] For these reasons, some scholars have doubted that any group lies behind these writings at all: instead, isolated individuals with mythological and cosmological interests wrote and read these works. The shared motifs and characters indicate merely that the writers borrowed from and elaborated on earlier texts.[59] Another proposal is that the Gnostics resembled what modern sociologists call an "audience cult." Like modern persons devoted to UFOs and other paranormal phenomena, Gnostics may have gathered occasionally to discuss their ideas and produced and read works that engaged with one another, but they did not look to Gnostic literature or a Gnostic community as their exclusive or primary mode of religious identity.[60]

At the other end of the spectrum, some historians envision a robust independent religious group with a full ritual life and complex development over centuries.[61] Based on a close analysis of the writings and the detection of layers of editing and revisions in some of them, John Turner has proposed a literary history of Gnostic works and a corresponding social history of the community in which they were produced. He imagines a group that emerged from originally separate circles devoted to Barbēlō and Seth; later joined with Christians who shared their interests in cosmology, biblical exegesis, and baptismal rituals; and then, as proto-orthodoxy gained strength, moved apart from Christianity and became more explicitly Platonist.[62] Elements of Turner's reconstruction seem very plausible—especially the later turn away from other Christians to more engagement with Platonist circles—but most scholars have been reluctant to be so precise about the history of the Gnostics.

Even if the evidence for a full-fledged social description and history of the Gnostics is lacking, there are several reasons to think that the Gnostic school of thought, at least at certain points in its history, consisted of a fairly well-defined community of persons for whom the group provided their primary mode of religious activity. Many of the Gnostic works describe or allude to a shared ritual—baptism—and they describe adherents with peculiar and distinctive terms—"seed of Seth," immovable race," "Those People." *The Revelation of Adam* and *The Gospel of Judas* include polemics against other religious people, differentiating an "us" from "them." The Gnostics must never have been very numerous, however, and as we shall see, the religious climate among persons devoted to Jesus became increasingly distant from their unique combination of Jewish, Christian, and Platonist traditions. Other Christian groups sought a more distinctively "Christian" identity, one more clearly different from "Judaism" and from traditional philosophy.

In this chapter, I have tried to sketch the basic beliefs and practices of the Gnostic school of thought, using only the evidence that the procedure that I described in Chapter 2 gathers. In this effort I have had to omit numerous details and leave aside the many problems of interpretation and consistency among the sources that scholars of "Gnosticism" find both fascinating and frustrating. Why, for example, do Zōstrianos and The Foreigner transpose two crucial constituent aeons of the Barbēlō while agreeing on nearly everything else?[63] Instead of exploring such detailed questions, we have seen that the overall Gnostic message is one of hope and salvation in Jesus, the incarnation of the divine savior, and that many of the Gnostic beliefs that modern people find most bizarre make sense both within the Gnostic worldview and within the spectrum of views that prevailed among intellectuals of the second and third centuries. The Gnostic myth, along with the rituals of baptism and ascent, represented a creative response to the life and message of Jesus of Nazareth. It was one attempt to craft a new religious movement out of the Jewish Bible and contemporary philosophy, in the light of the experiences of acquaintance that certain people had in the wake of Jesus' appearance. In retrospect, we can see it as one attempt to invent Christianity, a religion about Jesus Christ.

More than this, the Gnostic myth was one of the earliest such inventions of Christianity. Karen King points out that, as far as we know based on surviving literature, The Secret Book According to John "was the first Christian writing to formulate a comprehensive narrative of the nature of God, the origin of the world, and human salvation."[64] Although the Gnostic myth surely developed in interaction with other claims about Jesus and the God of Israel, we should not understand it primarily as a reaction to or rebellion against some "mainstream" Christian thought, which did not exist in the early second century. Instead, the Secret Book set the agenda for subsequent Christian theology. Confronted with the Gnostics' compelling narrative, other Christian intellectuals had to set out their own such comprehensive visions of God and humanity. Moreover, we should not think of the Gnostic school of thought as a movement that "lost" to other forms of Christianity; rather, the Gnostics were lively participants in an ongoing process of inventing and reinventing Christianity. In Chapters 4 and 5, I turn to that story of early Christian identity formation and explain why it is not the case that "the Church rejected Gnosticism."

# 4

## UNITY AND DIVERSITY IN
## SECOND-CENTURY ROME

I have argued that there was no widespread, multifaceted religious movement called "Gnosticism" in antiquity, but that there was a Gnostic school of thought, one group among the several that proclaimed that Jesus of Nazareth had brought salvation to human beings. In the second century, when the Gnostics emerged and became recognized as a community, Christians were still very few. When we speak of Gnostics as part of a "wider" Christianity, we must remind ourselves that Christianity itself was a small movement or collection of movements, hardly noticed in many places and in others still hard to distinguish from groups that we might identify as Jewish. Despite their small numbers, however, Christians were soon to be found in most major cities of the Roman Empire and in many midsized ones as well. Because there were so few of them, Christians were acutely aware of their differences.

From the start, Christians responded to the ministry and death of Jesus in various ways, but many of them also perceived the need to maintain not only unity with each other but also uniformity in belief and practice. An early example of this dynamic is the controversy over the circumcision of Gentile converts that erupted in the 40s, less than two decades after Jesus' death.[1] Some early believers, most notably Paul, believed that the death and resurrection of Jesus indicated that God would soon intervene in world history, bring a violent end to the current political order, and inaugurate a new kingdom of peace and justice. The arrival of this long-promised "day of the Lord," they believed, would inspire numerous Gentiles, non-Jews, to abandon their worship of idols and turn to the God of Israel. "Many people shall come and say, 'Come, let us go up to the mountain of the Lord, to the house of the God of

Jacob; that he may teach us his ways and that we may walk in his paths' " (Isaiah 2:3). In line with this conviction, Paul believed that the risen Jesus had called him to take the Gospel to Gentiles, and Paul founded several Christian communities in Asia Minor and Greece that consisted entirely of non-Jews. This development appears not to have been controversial among Jesus believers at first, for the inclusion of Gentiles was part of the scenario that many Jews believed would lead to the kingdom of God. But as the years rolled on, Jesus did not return and bring his kingdom, and Christian missionary activity among Jews began to lose steam. Some Jewish believers in Jesus began to argue that Gentile believers should convert fully to Judaism by being circumcised (if they were men) and observing the Jewish Law. Paul and his allies vigorously disagreed, arguing that Gentile believers would receive their salvation solely on the basis of their faith in Jesus and the God of Israel. This disagreement posed a serious threat to the unity of the movement: for example, could observant Jewish believers eat the same (nonkosher) foods as their Gentile coreligionists?

Leading Christians met in Jerusalem to discuss this question. The early Christian sources that report this meeting disagree about the nature of the meeting and precisely what was decided. According to the earlier report (that of Paul in Galatians 2), Paul met with several other prominent Christians privately, and they agreed that there would be two early Christian missions: one led by Paul and his colleagues, directed to Gentiles, and one led by Peter, James, and others, directed to Jews. Gentile converts would not be required to be circumcised, and Paul pledged to raise money among his Gentile communities for the poorer Jewish believers in the region of Jerusalem. It seems that the parties may not have had the same understanding about what this agreement meant for table fellowship between Jewish and Christian believers, for a major fight on this issue broke out shortly thereafter in Antioch. The later report (Acts 15) depicts a more public meeting, in which Peter and James took the lead in arguing against the circumcision of Gentile converts, who were instructed only to avoid sexual immorality and the eating of certain meats; there is no mention of two missions or of a collection. In comparison with Paul's report, the Acts account appears somewhat idealized and depicts Paul as clearly subordinate to the leaders based in Jerusalem, Peter and James. Paul's version, on the other hand, comes not from an objective eyewitness, but from a highly partisan participant, and so has its own shortcomings.

Whichever account one follows, this incident suggests that these early Christians were willing to tolerate some diversity within their movement, but not without limits. On the one hand, the Christians understood that Jewish and Gentile believers would retain their identities as Jews and Gentiles, and thus they would have different eating practices (perhaps to the point that they at times could not eat the same foods). Paul's report suggests even a toleration of specialized missions, targeted at differing ethnic or religious groups. On the other hand, the Christians did not want disagreement on such a fundamental question as how Gentiles could be included in the community of the elect, and they sought ways to ensure that even missions of very different characters would maintain solidarity (through Paul's collection, for example). Diversity was acceptable—but only to a point—and unity and fellowship were to be maintained.

This example does not tell the whole story, of course. For one thing, this dispute, as central as it is in the earliest surviving Christian literature, was not the only important controversy among the first believers, as Paul's letters demonstrate. We cannot be certain how other disagreements were settled, and there must have been still others that we do not know about at all. Moreover, even this disagreement did not engage all early Christians: other believers in Jesus may not have been aware of it or, if they were, may not have cared. We need to keep in mind that, when we consider struggles among Christians of the first two or three centuries, we are never dealing with disputes that involved Christians worldwide, as few as they were. Many arguments must have interested only small groups of believers who cared about the issues involved. It is, then, profitable to examine Christian unity and diversity in the early period at the local level, by looking at particular locales and disputes, without extrapolating from these specific studies to speaking of "Christianity" as a whole. In this chapter, I look at the city of Rome at the middle of the second century because we have good evidence for it, and we know that Gnostic teachings circulated there. The issues that Gnostic teachings raised—the identity of the God of Israel, the status of the Jewish Scriptures, acquaintance with the ultimate God—figure prominently in the works of early Roman Christian teachers.

The Jerusalem circumcision meeting should lead us to reflect also on the lack of any real coercive powers that any Christian leaders had to enforce decisions to which they agreed. In this case, it seems that harmony broke down rather quickly after the Jerusalem agreement: an argument flared in Antioch over whether Gentile and Jewish believers could eat the same foods, with the result that Paul broke off relations even with some of his former allies and became more of a lone apostle. In this period, only the sincere desire to remain in fellowship with fellow believers could motivate Christians to change their beliefs and practices to conform to those of others. For example, one early Christian author encouraged his addressees not to grant hospitality to traveling believers who did not share his teaching on the fleshly character of Jesus' body (2 John 7–10). Christian opponents of this author later used the same tactic, refusal of hospitality, against his own missionaries (3 John 10). Withdrawal of fellowship and heated rhetorical denunciations were the primary strategies available to Christians who wished to pressure fellow believers to change their ways. We should not expect that the situation in Rome in the 140s to 160s was much different.

As early as we can tell, Christians in Rome gathered and worshiped in several groups, without any single dominant "Church." We do not know how or when Christianity first came to Rome. Because it was the capital and largest city of the empire, and because travel was remarkably easy, multiple Christians could have made their way to it in the decades following the death and resurrection of Christ. And so there probably was not a single beginning to or founding apostle of Christianity in Rome, but several beginnings and founding missionaries. Our first piece of real evidence for Roman Christianity comes from the apostle Paul, who during the 50s of the first century wrote his now famous letter to the city's Gentile Christians. Paul had not yet been to Rome and was planning to visit it, and his letter served to introduce himself and his message to the believers there, who he hoped would provide him with the means to travel on to Spain. Phoebe, a deacon of the congregation in Cenchreae (a port of the Greek city Corinth) and a financial supporter of Paul, carried the letter to Rome, perhaps on a trip that she was making for business reasons (Romans 16:1–2).

Paul's Letter to the Romans reveals that in this early period the Roman Christian community consisted of several house churches and included many immigrants to Rome from the Greek-speaking East. The native language of Rome was Latin, but Paul wrote his letter in Greek, expecting the Christians would be able to read it. Even though Paul had never been to Rome, he was able to greet more than twenty Christians there by name in the conclusion of his letter. Some of these people he must have known only by reputation, but more of them he probably had met personally because they previously lived in the eastern Mediterranean, where Paul had spent his life to this point. We know this to be true in the cases of Prisca, Aquila, Epaenetus, Andronicus, and Junia because Paul mentions either his personal contact with them or their previous residence in eastern areas (16:3–7). Paul refers to at least three different house churches in Rome (16:5, 14–15), but there were likely more than these. The presence of immigrants to Rome and the existence of multiple house churches are likely related to one another. As immigrants came to Rome from different cities and regions of the East, they naturally congregated with other people from their home areas, who shared personal connections and similar traditions. Some of the house churches may have reflected this ethnic diversity, as Christians from, say, western Asia Minor worshiped together. Doubtless other house churches simply gathered Christians from certain areas of the city or reflected shared worship styles, personal affinities, or even social and economic levels. As Peter Lampe has described it, a state of "fractionation" characterized Roman Christianity from the start.[2]

But even in Paul's day, separation and diversity were not the entire story. To be sure, Paul's letter gives no indication that there is a central or primary Church community in Rome, much less a single individual who was the leader of Christians there. Paul may be aware that multiple house churches and ethnic diversity have led to or could lead to tensions among the city's Christians. He urges the Roman Christians not to judge one another in matters like eating practices and holiday observances, traditions that may reflect regional differences (14:1–12). Yet Paul assumes that the Roman Christians, despite their separation into smaller groups, know and interact with each other and think of themselves as "all God's beloved in Rome" (1:7). He expects them to circulate his letter among the groups, and even the concern about differences in eating practices indicates that Paul and the Roman Christians think of the Christians there as somehow a single community. We see, then, what Einar Thomassen has called a "tension between decentralizing and centralizing forces," a dynamic movement between unity and diversity that had complex and sometimes contradictory effects.[3]

This movement between unity and diversity characterized Roman Christianity well into the second century. Several factors continued to promote fractionation among Christians. Without any communal property of their own (despite the picture presented in Acts of the Apostles chapters 2–5), Christians continued to meet in private homes, which limited the number of people who could participate in any single meeting and also tied Christian groups to the household, where social factors like kinship, ethnicity, and wealth played an important role in identity. New immigrants continued to arrive in the city, reinforcing ethnic divisions and bringing a variety of local religious traditions. As the number of educated Christians grew, groups of Christian teachers and intellectuals arose, and theological differences joined social factors in contributing to Christian diversity. We can imagine that at some point in the second century a Christian teacher brought the teachings of the Gnostic school of thought to Rome, and the Gnostics joined the diverse stew of Romans who proclaimed salvation through Jesus Christ.

As fractionation persisted and even increased among the Roman Christians, they also developed ways to express their unity. When foreign Christians like Paul wrote to their coreligionists in Rome, they expected that the Romans had some shared way to receive such correspondence. By the turn of the second century, it appears that there may have been a secretary who was charged with handling correspondence for the entire Christian community: so we can understand the Clement of Rome who wrote a letter to Christians in Corinth in behalf of the Roman Christians in the late 90s (now known as *1 Clement*). Endeavors such as charity for the poor required ad hoc arrangements of cooperation and perhaps the appointment of shared officers. The separate house-based congregations developed the custom of sending token portions of the Eucharist to each other as expressions of solidarity. It seems that there were occasional citywide meetings of leaders called presbyters (elders), teachers, and even bishops, but it is not clear how representative or frequent these meetings were or how much power they had.

A Roman Christian around the year 150 would have had a variety of religious options available to her. She could worship at one of several house churches, which may have featured a diversity of worship practices and theological ideas. She could deepen her understanding of Christian teachings by studying with one of the city's several philosophers who taught about the Jewish Scriptures and Greek and Roman philosophical traditions in light of the new revelation in Jesus. One of the options available to her must have been the Gnostic school of thought. We can explore how the Gnostics and other Christians interacted with each other by focusing on three prominent Roman Christians who most likely knew about the Gnostics' teaching and who came into conflict with other Christians over the meaning of the new faith: Marcion, Valentinus, and

Justin. We shall learn not only that there was no single Church in Rome that could reject "Gnosticism," but also that even a model of conflict between "proto-orthodoxy" and a variety of "other groups" fails to do justice to the complexity of Christian diversity on the ground. The Gnostics did not lose a war; rather, they were participants in a lively and often contested multilateral process of defining and redefining what Christianity might be.

## Marcion: Scriptures and Withdrawal of Fellowship

Marcion, a member of a wealthy shipowning family from Sinope in Pontus (Asia Minor), arrived in Rome around 140. He made an immediate splash among Roman Christians by making a substantial donation (reportedly 200,000 sesterces) to a common fund, presumably for charity to the poor. Not much later, however, Marcion was making waves in Christian circles for other reasons—his religious teachings and his proposals for placing Christianity on a more standardized basis. Eventually Marcion would sever relations with other Roman Christians, who gave him his money back, and he would start his own international network of churches. Despite his success as a church organizer, Marcion's writings have been lost. To reconstruct his teachings, historians must rely on the reports of his enemies. Still, the most important points in his version of Christianity seem clear enough. Marcion's story demonstrates the limits of tolerance among early Christian groups and the importance of sacred writings to new Christian understandings of truth.[4]

There is no evidence that Marcion had contact with Gnostics or knew the Gnostic myth, but such seems highly probable, given how small the Christian subculture was. In any event, Marcion's teaching presented a strikingly streamlined alternative to the Gnostic myth, while speaking to some of the same concerns. The Gnostics considered the Jewish Scriptures a flawed witness to a demonic god; still, with revelatory guidance from the higher powers, the biblical texts could furnish insight into salvation history. Marcion, in contrast, rejected the Jewish Scriptures as irrelevant to Christians, indeed contradictory to the Gospel. When Marcion compared the teachings of Jesus as he found them in the Gospel of Luke and the letters of Paul with the teachings of the Septuagint, he found contradiction after contradiction. Where Jesus preached love and forgiveness, the God of Israel appeared to recommend merely justice and retribution. Where Paul denied that Christians needed to follow the Jewish Law, the Jewish Scriptures considered righteous only those who practiced that Law. Christians other than the Gnostics had noticed these problems, which they solved in a variety of ways. Some Christians posited a development in God's dealings with humanity: the Law had served its purpose by leading people to Christ and need not be followed in all its details any longer. Others interpreted problematic passages symbolically and not literally: God did not mean for people to follow his prohibitions of certain foods literally; rather, such commandments conveyed more general ethical or religious principles in symbolic ways. Marcion took neither of these paths, and instead concluded that the God of Israel simply could not be related to Jesus and the Gospel at all, much less the Father of Jesus.

Marcion's view of the creator god differed sharply from that of the Gnostics. The Gnostics considered Ialdabaōth to be arrogant, foolish, and even demonic; his actions toward human beings are at the least amoral and more probably immoral. And yet Ialdabaōth does not lack any connection to the higher, truly divine God; rather, he is a kind of disfigured offspring of true divinity, and his distant awareness of true spiritual reality enables him to create this imperfect universe. Marcion's creator god, by contrast, is not evil, but unrelentingly just. His moral demands on human beings are not really wrong—certainly people should not kill, and they should honor their parents—but he has set the bar so high, and his punishments are so severe, that mere mortal human beings cannot hope to avoid eternal damnation. His severe and uncompromising regime resembles that of authoritarian earthly rulers.[5] Unlike Ialdabaōth, this creator does not have a clear relationship to the ultimate God, whom Marcion calls the Stranger. The Stranger is a divine being who is utterly transcendent and, until the arrival of Jesus, unknown to this created order. He resembles the Gnostics' Invisible Spirit, for Marcion shared the widespread Platonizing assumption of a perfect, transcendent God. The Stranger God's great compassion led him to send his Son, Jesus, to meet the retributive demand of the creator god and so to save human beings. Jesus was not actually a human being of flesh and blood like ours—he only appeared to be so—rather, he was an emissary from the Stranger God, sent to offer us that God's grace and forgiveness.

Marcion drew significant conclusions about Christian practice from his beliefs. First, he proposed a new Christian Bible: Christians would not use the Jewish Scriptures as sacred writings at all, but instead follow only a single Gospel (similar to but not identical with the Gospel of Luke) and a collection of Paul's letters (not including all those that ended up in the New Testament). Because both the Gospel known to Marcion and Paul's letters contained passages that suggested that the God of Israel was in fact the Father of Jesus Christ, Marcion edited these texts to remove what he considered later interpolations. In undertaking this kind of editorial work, Marcion did not differ much from many other Christians. The authors of the Gospels of Matthew and Luke, for example, had revised the Gospel of Mark in creating their works. As a scholar, Marcion sought to recover the original form of sacred documents that had suffered corruption. Nor is it likely that Marcion was unique in using only one Gospel, which was probably the practice of most Christian communities before the late second century. Second, he urged Christians to protest the oppressive world order of the creator god by abstaining from sex and from the consumption of meat and wine.[6] Finally, he believed in an organized Church structure with the rituals of baptism and the Eucharist (celebrated without wine).

Of these proposals it is the first that distinguishes Marcion most clearly from the Gnostics. The Gnostics maintained a conflicted engagement with Genesis and the sacred writings of the Jews, and their modes of teaching and writing drew openly on a long tradition of Jewish apocalypticism. In this way, the Gnostics demonstrated their roots in forms of Judaism, even as they rejected some of the core beliefs of most Jews. Marcion, on the other hand, presented Christianity as something entirely new, rather than as a growth from Jewish tradition, although, to be sure, his exposition of Christianity required Jewish tradition as its foil.

Marcion appears to have been something of an entrepreneur, both commercially and religiously, and it seems that he was eager to bring other Christian groups in Roman into line with his reforms. At least some Christian communities found Marcion's teachings disturbing, and at times they broke off fellowship with him, most likely by refusing to exchange tokens of the Eucharist, only to reinstate it again. Finally, in the summer of 144, Marcion asked to meet with the city's "presbyters and teachers" and to use a passage similar to Luke 5:36–37 (putting "new wine" into "old wineskins") as the basis for a discussion of his teachings. The meeting did not go well, and fellowship between Marcion and his fellow Roman Christians came to a definitive end. His generous contribution was returned to him. Precisely who first withdrew fellowship is not clear: it may have been Marcion who "excommunicated" other

Christians. But this result did not stop Marcion, who quickly developed a network of churches that spread across the Mediterranean and lasted for centuries.[7]

As Peter Lampe and Einar Thomassen have argued, we learn from Marcion's experience that during the middle decades of the second century the fractionated Roman Christian community generally tolerated diversity among its different groups. Marcion's complete rejection of the Jewish Scriptures and his asceticism distinguished his community clearly from other Christian circles, and yet there was no decisive break between Marcion and other Christians until Marcion himself sought to bring other communities into line with his teachings. Marcion upset the delicate balance between unity and diversity by seeking to impose greater unity and uniformity among Roman Christians than they wanted. And, of course, the beliefs and practices on which he sought to base that unity were not acceptable to other Christians. Both Marcion's theological difference and his push for unity led to withdrawal of fellowship. The withdrawal of communion could be an effective means of differentiating one's own Christian group from another, but in Marcion's case it was hardly effective in eliminating one's rival groups.

## Valentinus: Adaptation of the Gnostic Myth and Personal Authority

In contrast to Marcion, there can be no doubt that the Christian philosopher Valentinus had contact with the Gnostics and was aware of their myth. Irenaeus reports that "Valentinus adapted the fundamental principles of the so-called Gnostic school of thought to his own kind of system."[8] We are right to be suspicious of this claim because it is Irenaeus's strategy to denigrate Christians whose views he rejects by portraying them as the intellectual successors of other false Christians. Still, an exhaustive study of Valentinus's surviving works by Anne McGuire confirms Irenaeus's report.[9] Valentinus was not a Gnostic, and it appears that he took some pains to distinguish his views from Gnostic teachings, which were only one among many sources of his own thought. But he did not simply reject those teachings; rather, he created a new myth that was less elaborate and more centered on Christ. In addition, he eschewed the pseudonymous apocalyptic mode of Gnostic writing and instead claimed his own visionary insight and philosophical authority.[10]

Valentinus taught in Rome from the late 130s until the 160s, nearly thirty years. According to a much later account (by Epiphanius of Salamis in the fourth century), Valentinus was born in Egypt and educated in Alexandria. Although we cannot be certain of this claim, there are several reasons that it is likely to be true, among them that it is Clement of Alexandria who has preserved many of the excerpts from otherwise lost writings of Valentinus.[11] From these writings it is clear that Valentinus received a very good education and was well read in Platonic, biblical, Jewish, and Christian literature. In Rome Valentinus emerged as a prominent Christian teacher. Several of his students became important Christian theologians in their own right, most prominently Ptolemy of Rome, and a Valentinian school of Christian thought (with two distinct branches) continued well into the fourth century. According to one report, a Christian group in Rome came close to electing Valentinus their bishop. Rival Christian teachers criticized Valentinus and his students sharply, but there is no evidence that Valentinus himself was ever formally condemned by any organized Christian group with power to enforce its judgment.[12] After the mid-160s Valentinus disappears into the fog of history, and we have no information about his later life and death.

Discovering what Valentinus taught is a formidable task, and scholars disagree about many important points. Unlike in Marcion's case, where nothing of what he wrote appears to survive, we have some fragmentary quotations from Valentinus's lost works and an entire (if short) poem. It seems almost certain that the anonymous sermon *The Gospel of Truth* can be attributed to Valentinus, and a portion of Methodius of Olympus's *On Free Will* may represent his views.[13] Irenaeus provides an extremely brief summary of the myth that Valentinus taught: because Valentinus adapted the teachings of the Gnostics and because Irenaeus's real targets are the students of Valentinus, he seems concerned to present only highlights of Valentinus's doctrines, rather than the complete myth (if there was one). With so little to work with, scholars debate how much they can use the teachings of Valentinus's followers, especially Ptolemy, to reconstruct his thought. For example, did Valentinus's myth include a single divine figure of Wisdom ("the Mother"), as the Gnostic myth did and Irenaeus's summary suggests, or two manifestations of Wisdom (a "higher" and a "lower" Wisdom), as his student Ptolemy taught? However these questions are answered, we can see the ways in which Valentinus responded to Gnostic teachings by transforming them, rather than by rejecting them outright.

For example, Valentinus took from the Gnostics the idea that the created material world is the result of some sort of mistake or error by a feminine figure. He did not, however, portray this world in unrelentingly negative terms, but stressed its dependence on God and its ultimate meaninglessness, even unreality. According to Irenaeus, Valentinus agreed with the Gnostics that the ultimate God unfolds himself into a series of emanations, one of which "revolted" or "turned away" and "became lacking," resulting in the generation of the material world. In *The Gospel of Truth,* this turning away from knowledge of the ultimate God is personified as Error, the feminine origin of materiality. Valentinus's Error combines and adapts the figures of Wisdom and Ialdabaōth in Gnostic myth.[14] Because the material world has its origin in error or ignorance, it is ultimately not real, for the only true reality is God, and other beings are real only to the extent that they participate in God through knowledge of him. God, then, underlies and is present in and with all things that truly are. Valentinus's poem or hymn "Summer Harvest" evokes the dependence on God of everything that exists:

I see in spirit that all are hung
I know in spirit that all are borne
Flesh hanging from soul
Soul clinging to air
Air hanging from upper atmosphere
Crops rushing forth from the deep
A babe rushing forth from the womb.[15]

Valentinus's strong emphasis on the immanence of God differentiates him from the Gnostics and supplements the Platonist distinction between spirit and matter with a kind of Stoic pantheism (although the Stoics were materialists and would not accept that matter is not ultimately real).[16]

Two fragments show Valentinus in dialogue with Gnostic accounts of the creation of Adam.[17] In one passage, Valentinus considers how it is that statues, paintings, and other artifacts become representations of gods and thus "objects of awe" for the human beings that made them. He adduces as a parallel example the creation of Adam by angels: Adam's speech terrified the angels because it indicated the presence of a seed of higher essence deposited in him by the Word of God. Adam represented the divine archetypal human being in a powerful way, so that the angels were amazed and frightened. Valentinus inherited from the Gnostics the ideas that Adam was created by lower divine beings, that the higher divine power placed within him a seed of divinity without the knowledge of the lower creators, and that Adam's speech or upright stature displayed his superiority to his creators. But Valentinus's creating angels are not as demonic and hostile as are Ialdabaōth and the rulers of Gnostic myth, and Valentinus emphasizes the divine presence that makes up for the imperfection of the material creation. Moreover, it appears that the divine agent who transmits divine essence to humanity is not Wisdom or Forethought, but the Son or Word of God, whom Valentinus refers to also as God's "name." The lower angels may have failed to reproduce the eternal form of divine humanity in creating the material Adam, "yet the name completed the lack within the act of modeling." Although he accepted Gnostic ideas that the material creation is highly imperfect and the work of lower beings, Valentinus reduced the antagonism between humanity and its creators, and he stressed the work of God's Word to complete or fill the imperfection of materiality.

In comparison to the Gnostics, Valentinus placed Jesus Christ much more at the center of his thought. The Word of God is a prominent aeon in the divine fullness as Valentinus envisioned it, and according to one ancient source, Valentinus saw a vision in which the Word appeared to him in the form of an infant.[18] He had such a strong sense of the divinity of Jesus that he considered the possibility that Jesus' body did not digest foods in the same manner as did ordinary human bodies.[19] The sermon *The Gospel of Truth* includes an extensive meditation on the relationship between the Son and the Father. As the name of the Father, the Son reveals the Father to created beings. Jesus' crucifixion is the climactic moment of divine self-revelation: "He was nailed to a tree and became fruit of the Father's acquaintance. Yet it did not cause ruin because it was eaten. Rather, to those who ate of it, it gave the possibility that whoever he discovered within himself might be joyful in the discovery of him. And as for him, they discovered him within them—the inconceivable, uncontained, the Father, who is perfect, who created the entirety."[20] Here the crucifixion, as the moment in which *gnōsis* of God becomes possible, looks backward to the Fall in Eden and forward to the Christian Eucharist. By eating the body of Christ, Christians participate in the crucifixion of Christ and gain knowledge of God and of themselves, for God is within them as the inconceivable origin of all that truly is. In contrast to the Eden story, this knowledge brings joy and life, not regret and ruin. The Gnostic author of *The Gospel of Judas* mocked the Eucharist as ignorant worship of a false God, but Valentinus celebrated it as the means of joyous discovery of God and self.

Valentinus differed from the Gnostics as well in how he presented his teaching as authoritative. The Gnostics, we have seen, attributed their literary works to authoritative figures of the past, whether very distant (Adam, Zoroaster) or more recent (John the Apostle), and these works were mostly revelations from divine beings. Even though it must have been the Gnostic authors themselves who received the visionary insights that they sought to communicate in their literature, they did not claim these insights for themselves, but presented their works as wisdom from above or from antiquity. Valentinus, however, invoked his own mystical experience as the basis for his teachings. As we have seen, he reportedly had a visionary experience in which the Word of God appeared to him as an infant.[21] In *The Gospel of Truth,* he announced, "I have been in the place of repose"; true children of God, he said, "speak of the light that is perfect and full of the Father's seed."[22] For Valentinus, the Christians who have gained acquaintance of God have discovered themselves, for they are in God and God is in them: such Christians can speak the wisdom that all God-inspired philosophy teaches, which is "the utterances that come from the heart, the law that is written in the heart."[23] They are themselves "texts of truth, which speak and know only themselves."[24] The visionary insight that Valentinus claimed was available to any who follow the path of knowledge that Jesus has made available.

According to Clement of Alexandria, Valentinus's students promoted his authority in another way. They asserted that he had been a student of Theudas, who had been a disciple of Paul.[25] If this report is true, then Valentinus presented himself not only as the recipient of an extraordinary level of the insight that Christianity makes accessible to all, but also as a trained philosopher. An ancient teacher often legitimated his or her teaching by producing an intellectual pedigree that traced his or her academic tradition through a succession of brilliant teachers back to a founder whom many others admired, such as Plato or Zeno or, for Christians, Paul or Jesus himself. This succession was sometimes the conduit for a secret oral tradition that contained doctrines more advanced than those found in available written texts of the school.[26] Rival teachers competed with one another, often through personal attacks on another's lifestyle and academic pedigree; this kind of polemic is not surprising, given the personal nature of the teacher's authority.[27] The teacher's authority could continue after death through the dissemination of his or her philosophical treatises and scriptural commentaries and the publication of idealizing biographies by his or her students. In Valentinus's case, his disciples and their communities seem to have conducted worship using hymns that Valentinus had composed, and to have drawn from and commented on his writings.[28] In distinction, then, to the Gnostics and in competition with rival versions of Christianity, Judaism, and philosophy in general, Valentinus cloaked himself in a highly personal type of authority, combining visionary insight and an impressive academic lineage.

Although we know that Valentinus and his teachings aroused opposition from some other Christian leaders, Valentinus himself evinced an optimistic openness, even missionary zeal, toward others, whether they were Christians outside his immediate community of followers or not Christians at all. "Unto those who are weary give repose; and awaken those who wish to arise," he exhorted his followers. "For it is you who are unsheathed intelligence." On the other hand, he counseled neglect of those who had fallen away from the group: "Do not focus your attention upon others, that is, ones whom you have expelled."[29] It is unlikely that Valentinus saw himself and his followers as a special or elite group within a wider Christian community; rather, he believed that he was teaching a message for all people, or as he might put it, for everyone whose name is written in the book of the living.[30] Indeed, unity and harmony are major themes of *The Gospel of Truth:* the aeonic emanations of the Father enjoy a gracious unity with each other and with God, who is their completion; only ignorance of each other and of God disrupts this unity. The analogy with human beings (themselves emanations of the Father) is clear: "For now their affairs are dispersed . . . It is by acquaintance that all will purify themselves out of multiplicity into unity . . . it is fitting for us to meditate upon the entirety, so that this house might be holy and quietly intent on unity."[31] Valentinus then tells a parable about how the coming of the Word causes a great disturbance among a set of jars in a house: some break, some are found to be empty, some are full. Einar Thomassen has plausibly suggested that this parable can be read as an allegory for how Christians groups responded in diverse ways to the stirring message of saving *gnōsis* that Valentinus offered.[32]

Valentinus's near election as a bishop (if true) indicates that at least some Roman Christians outside his own school acknowledged him as a gifted Christian teacher, even if others condemned his views. We shall see in Chapter 5 that the later school of Christian thought that was indebted to him would have a subtle and complex relationship to other Christian groups, but Valentinus's vision was one of unity. He himself was never condemned for his teachings both because many Christians found them acceptable and because at the time there was no central Christian authority that could have issued and enforced such a condemnation. Recall that no central authority condemned Marcion, either. Rather, he and other Christians discontinued fellowship after a meeting that he initiated. Valentinus illustrates another possible response to the Gnostic school of thought—adaptation and inclusion. He drew insights from the Gnostic myth, adapted it to his own views, and articulated a visionary method of unity that sought to include all Christians. His own personal authority of insight and learning gave his message its persuasive power.

## Justin Martyr: Heresiology and Rejection of Gnostic Myth

Like Marcion and Valentinus, the Christian teacher Justin came to Rome from elsewhere. He was born in Flavia Neapolis in Palestine (modern-day Nablus) to a pagan family. At some point he became a Christian, but Justin presented that decision as the natural step in his pursuit of philosophy, the culmination of a search for truth and wisdom that had led him to other schools of thought, including the Pythagoreans and the Platonists. "Thus it is I am now a philosopher"—so he concluded the story of his journey to Christianity—and he looked the part by wearing the distinctive cloak of the working philosopher.[33] In Rome Justin rented an apartment above a bath, where he taught anyone who wished to study Christian philosophy with him. As H. Gregory Snyder has pointed out, "A location over or around a bathhouse would have offered several distinct advantages to a teacher such as Justin: relatively plentiful amounts of light, availability of important services, the status and convenience of being located near a local landmark, and . . . a generous amount of quiet, relative to other possible locations."[34] Like Valentinus, then, Justin was an independent teacher of Christianity whose claim to authority depended on his learning and charisma, not on an official position in a Church.

Unlike Valentinus, however, Justin did not find in the Gnostic myth insights that he could adapt to his own views; instead, he rejected

Gnostic teachings and those of Valentinus and Marcion, and in the process he helped to invent what we now call "heresy." As we have seen, the Gnostics were known as the "Gnostic school of thought" or *gnōstikē hairesis*. *Hairesis* was a mostly neutral term that indicated that a field of study, such as medicine, included within it different schools of thought: a *hairesis* shared allegiance to a set of doctrines or to an original teacher. In religious or philosophical settings, *hairesis* could also have a purely descriptive sense: the Jewish author Josephus claimed to follow "the *hairesis* of the Pharisees," and Clement of Alexandria argued that "the most accurate *gnōsis* and the truly best *hairesis* reside in the only true and ancient Church."[35] Shared intellectual heritage might be all that held a school together socially. That is, the term need not imply an organized social group that held meetings and had a strong sense of membership. But we have seen indications that at least some Gnostics did in fact form a social group with shared rituals and a sense of communal identity. Different schools of thought within a field like medicine would certainly argue with each other, and the polemics could become heated and personal, but the existence of different ways of thinking about medicine was neither surprising nor unusual.

From the earliest years of Christian history, however, some Christians were aware of diversity and disagreements within their movement, and they sought to contain such divisions, which contradicted the notion that they formed a single body of Christ. Paul condemned "factions" *(haireseis)* among Christians as "works of the flesh" (Galatians 5:19–20). Paul lamented that when Christians in Corinth gathered for the Lord's Supper there were "divisions" *(schismata)* among them, although he admitted that there may be some value in such quarrels: "There have to be factions *(haireseis)* among you, for only so will it become clear who among you are genuine" (1 Corinthians 11:18–19). The divisions among the Corinthian Christians that Paul condemns here appear to have been based in social and economic differences rather than on different teachings, and so here a *hairesis* simply means a "faction."

In the second century, however, some Christian authors tied the existence of factions more closely to differences in doctrines. The author of 2 Peter depicted the dying Apostle Peter as predicting the appearance of "false teachers, who will secretly bring in destructive *haireseis*," meaning here perhaps "ways of thinking" rather than "divisions" (2 Peter 2:1). Ignatius of Antioch praised the Christians in Ephesus because "you all live according to truth and no *hairesis* exists among you; rather, you do not even listen to anyone unless he speaks about Jesus Christ in truth" (*To the Ephesians* 6.2). He exhorted the Trallian Christians to "make use only of Christian food and avoid any foreign plant, which is *hairesis*" (*To the Trallians* 6.1). These authors attribute factionalism to false teaching, that which is both opposed to the truth and foreign to Christianity (as they define it). Without using the term *hairesis,* the author of 1 Timothy in the New Testament attributed some false teachings to demons (1 Timothy 4:1), and he warned against "what is falsely called *gnōsis*" (6:20). (From this phrase Irenaeus got the title of his book.) Before Justin, then, some Christians had associated *haireseis* with factions and false teachings, and others had suggested that demons could inspire erroneous doctrines. No one, however, had put these ideas into a single package, so to speak.

It is not clear how much of this previous Christian literature was known to Justin, but the imagery and associations that they contain appear in his new conception of "heresy." He reports that Jesus had predicted, "There shall be divisions *(schismata)* and factions *(haireseis)*."[36] This saying does not appear in any of the Gospels that we know and may be a conflation of Paul's statements about "divisions" and "factions" in 1 Corinthians. In any event, when he used the term *hairesis*, Justin combined the philosophical concept of "school of thought"—and its associated ideas of an original teacher and shared doctrines—with the Christian distrust of "factions" and diverse teachings as "foreign" and even demonic. Here no "school of thought" could be the source of Christian truth, nor could one call the true Christian Church a "school of thought," as Clement did. In fact, Justin wrote a now lost work entitled *Against All the Schools of Thought That Have Arisen* and another book specifically against Marcion (also lost).[37] With Justin the essential elements of the Christian idea of "heresy" and the practice of heresiology fell into place.

Justin argued that "schools of thought" or, as we may now put it, "heresies" were not really Christian, even if their adherents may have claimed to be so. People like Marcion, Valentinus, and their followers may have called themselves Christians, but Justin and those like him called them by the names of the men who originated their teachings. They were not "Christians," but "Marcionites," "Valentinians," and so forth.[38] Justin admitted that such people not only called themselves Christians but also were recognized as such by others. Still, he said, they are not really Christians, but "godless and impious members of a school of thought *(hairesiōtai)*." True Christians, by contrast, are "completely right-thinking."[39] This distinction between what people or things *are called* and what they *really are* is a key part of Justin's notion of heresy: heretics simply are not what they claim to be or what naïve others may think they are, that is, Christians.[40] They have their origin not in Christ, but in later human teachers, or rather in the demons who inspired those teachers.[41]

Like Valentinus, Justin did not reject non-Christian philosophy but believed that the classic works of Greek and Roman culture contained truths that are also found in Christianity. Valentinus seems to have attributed this phenomenon to the interior illumination that he believed came from acquaintance with God, what he called "the law that is written in the heart." And thus "publicly available books" often teach the same things as Christian books.[42] Justin, however, claimed that the Word of God, even before his incarnation in Jesus, was partially available to certain wise teachers in the form of "seeds." The teachings of Plato, Socrates, and others approximate those of Christ, for each spoke according to the partial knowledge that the Word made available to him. The entire Word was present in Christ, and thus (true) Christians possess the entirety of truth and can claim as their own whatever right teaching non-Christian philosophers have espoused.[43] Although the argument is different, Justin's approach to the discovery of truth is remarkably similar to that of Valentinus: reading and learning from a variety of traditions and texts, both men were open to discerning within them the revelation of the Word. Both were creating a new Christian philosophy, casting their intellectual nets widely to gather truth from the best of what came before.[44]

While Valentinus's net included the Gnostic myth, Justin's did not: his concept of heresy portrayed any Christians who held a low opinion of the Creator God (as he put it, those who "blaspheme the Creator of the universe") as demonically inspired counterfeits both of wholly true Christianity (taught by Justin) and its partially true relative, non-Christian philosophy.[45] Both heresy and philosophy, in his view, are varied imitations of Christianity, but while philosophy's diversity and approximation to Christianity results from its origin in only partial seeds of the Word—it's almost, but not quite Christianity—heresy comes from the demons. The demons, Justin explained, not only oppose Christ and his present-day followers, but also fought against those persons before Christ, like Socrates, who spoke the truth by the Word.[46] In Justin's view, such heretics as Marcion and Valentinus were only the latest means by which the evil spirits were doing battle against the Word of God. Certainly the Gnostics would find the idea of demonic rulers opposing the work of the true God familiar, although they would be alarmed to find themselves portrayed as demonically motivated.

Justin developed his idea of heresy explicitly in response to Christian diversity, something that he viewed with somewhat more subtlety than my discussion thus far might indicate. Justin discusses other disagreements among Christians in his *Dialogue with Trypho,* which depicts a fictitious conversation between Justin and a Jew named Trypho. In one instance Trypho himself notes that there are Christians who disagree with Justin about whether it is acceptable to eat meat that had been sacrificed to pagan gods. The fact of Christian diversity is so clear that Justin felt compelled to include it in his text and even to portray an outsider as observing it. In another passage Trypho expresses skepticism that Justin honestly believes that the resurrection of the dead will be followed by a period during which resurrected Christians and pre-Christian Israelites will live in a reconstructed Jerusalem on earth, perhaps because he knows that it is not a widely shared belief even among Christians. In the first case, Justin bluntly condemns the eating of sacrificial meat as a demonically inspired practice and includes Christians who endorse it among those who blaspheme the Creator God and so are false Christians or heretics. Here Justin takes the hard-line position of the author of Revelation (2:20) rather than the more nuanced view of Paul (1 Corinthians 8:4–6). In the second case, Justin admits that "many pure and pious Christians" do not share his belief about a post-resurrection existence in Jerusalem. But then he brands as heretical those Christians who deny the resurrection of the dead and instead believe that the soul ascends to heaven immediately at death: such Christians also blaspheme the God of Israel. In any event, Christians who are "entirely right-thinking" agree with Justin on all the particulars of the resurrection.[47] Here we see that Justin did not consider every point of doctrine a matter of "Christianity" versus "heresy" or the teaching of the Word versus that of the demons. Rather, it was blasphemy against the Creator, the God of Israel, that indicated heresy.

Justin's focus on the status of the Creator God as the flashpoint of heresy is understandable when we consider that Justin's teaching about God was not completely different from the beliefs of his opponents. The Gnostics, Marcion, Valentinus, and Justin all agreed that to speak of only one God is too simple. All believed that the ultimate God was remarkably transcendent and not really accessible to human knowledge and that therefore some lower mediating divinity was required. The Gnostics, Valentinus, and Justin all used the term Word *(logos)* among others to identify this mediating God, who interacts with the created order in a way that the highest God cannot. It was, then, necessary for Justin to highlight as sharply as he could how his teaching differed from these other Christians, and he seized on the status of the Creator. Marcion, the Gnostics, and Valentinus stressed the imperfection of the Creator: he is ignorant and hostile to humanity (Gnostics), or unrelentingly righteous and lacking in mercy (Marcion), or simply lower and less spiritual than the ultimate God (Valentinus). In contrast, although Justin insisted that the Word was "another" God, one who was distinct in number from the ultimate God, and who could engage in such lesser activities as appearing in a burning bush, he pointedly referred to the high God as "the Creator of all things."[48] The Word may have been God the Father's agent in making and guiding the universe,[49] but the creation is the work of the ultimate God. Justin's "heresy" marked difference where others might have seen similarity.

Justin condemned the Gnostics, Marcion, Valentinus, and others as heretics, false Christians, but he had no authority to enforce his views on other Christian groups in Rome. Justin was just one of a variety of teachers and other leaders who offered insight into God and the human condition in light of the death and resurrection of Jesus. Indeed, it would be wrong to imagine Justin defending some preexisting thing such as "Christianity" or "the Church" against heretics and pagan critics. Instead, although he claimed to teach truth that was old as creation, Justin, just like the Gnostics, Marcion, and Valentinus, was creating (or recreating) something new, his own version of the new/old philosophy, Christianity. In so doing he debated with other reinventors of Christianity, disagreeing politely with some (the "pure and pious Christians" who held different views of the future eschatological era) and rejecting others as not Christians at all (the "heretics" who held different views of the Creator God). But Justin did not represent an official Church or a "mainstream" Christianity, nor did he have any power to define Christianity or its doctrines other than his ability to persuade others.

Later Christians identified Justin as "orthodox" and Marcion and Valentinus as "heretics"; modern scholars, trying to avoid such language and the value judgments it implies, nonetheless have usually called Justin "proto-orthodox" and Marcion and Valentinus representatives of "Gnosticism." But such categories fail to capture the complexity of these early Roman Christians. On the one hand, the teachings of Marcion and Valentinus differed significantly from those of the Gnostics and of each other, and neither considered himself a member of "the immovable race" or "the seed of Seth"; in contrast to the Gnostics, they celebrated varying forms of a Christian Eucharist and did not observe a baptism of five seals. On the other hand, Justin can hardly be distinguished from either Valentinus or Marcion as clearly as the label "proto-orthodox" implies. Justin shared Marcion's intolerance for certain alternative Christian views, and he even more closely resembled Valentinus: both were independent Christian philosophers who offered their learning and insight to interested students; both appreciated the presence of Christian truth in non-Christian philosophy; and both placed at the center of their thought the Son or Word of God, who alone reveals the Father and became incarnate in Jesus. The vehemence with which Justin denounced Marcion and Valentinus as "heretics" is an indication of their similarity to him as much as their distance.

There were very few Christians in Rome in the 140s, but despite or perhaps because of their small numbers, the differences among them appeared to some of them to loom large as they sought a balance between unity and diversity. Marcion, Valentinus, and Justin developed a set of responses to the Gnostic sect and/or each other that enabled them to fashion their own identities as religious leaders within not only the wider Christian community but also the larger pluralistic religious and philosophical culture of Rome. These strategies included outright rejection of alternative views through the rhetoric of heresy (Justin), withdrawal of fellowship and the establishment of self-consciously independent communities (Marcion), adaptation of the Gnostic myth and greater integration of it with other Christian literature (Valentinus), and more personal or philosophical modes of authority and legitimation of teaching (Valentinus and Justin). Christians in the following decades would borrow, develop, and augment these strategies as they sought to invent and reinvent Christianity in part by differentiating themselves from competing versions of it.

# 5

## STRATEGIES OF SELF-DIFFERENTIATION

No matter their diversity and disagreements, early Christians liked to imagine themselves as a single community spread across the world. The power of this self-understanding animates one of the earliest surviving Christian inscriptions, the epitaph of Abercius, bishop of Hieropolis in Phrygia, Asia Minor. Dating no later than 216 and perhaps as early as the 190s, the text commemorates the life of "Abercius, disciple of the holy shepherd," in the first person. Abercius relates that during his life he traveled from his home in Asia Minor as far west as Rome in Italy and as far east as Nisibis and the Euphrates River in Mesopotamia. Everywhere he went, Abercius says, he found "kindred spirits," those who shared the same faith and celebrated the same Eucharist of bread and wine. He asks that those who see his tomb and share his convictions pray on his behalf. Abercius provides a touching and dramatic witness to the unity of Christians spread throughout the Roman Empire.[1]

Ironically, however, the Christians in his home region of Phrygia did not enjoy complete unity. Christians there disagreed about the legitimacy of a prophetic movement that had begun in the 160s when the Christians Montanus, Maximilla, and Priscilla claimed to receive new revelations from the Holy Spirit. Eventually known as the New Prophecy, this movement attracted many Christians with its emphasis on moral discipline, prophetic inspiration, and hope for a coming New Jerusalem. In Abercius's day, some adherents of New Prophecy followed a leader named Miltiades. Many bishops, however, denounced the New Prophecy as false, even demonically inspired. One learned opponent of the movement even dedicated an entire treatise refuting it to Bishop Abercius. Montanus, the author argued, prophesied "in a way that conflicted with the practice of the Church handed down generation by generation from the beginning." Maximilla's prophecies, he noted, had not come true.[2] So Abercius, whose epitaph would later celebrate the presence of like-minded Christians in places as distant as Rome and Nisibis, also found himself at the center of Christian disharmony and conflict.[3]

Abercius's experience demonstrates that the tension between unity and diversity that we observed in mid-second-century Rome was not unique to the Christian communities in the imperial capital. Abercius, too, expected Christians wherever they lived to share certain beliefs and practices, and he valued the solidarity among all those who followed "the holy shepherd," Christ. And yet there were limits to Abercius's fellowship with other Christians—if we assume that he was sympathetic to the treatise against the New Prophecy that was dedicated to him. Abercius's correspondent declared that he, Abercius, and others like them adhered to "the true faith," while Christians who accepted the prophecies of Montanus and his colleagues constituted a "recent schismatic heresy." The author offered several specific criticisms of the Phrygian prophets, including the ecstatic manner in which they prophesied and their lack of prophetic successors. The writing of the treatise suggests, of course, that the line between "the true faith" and the "recent schismatic heresy" was not so clear; indeed, the author complains that the Church in Ancyra in Galatia is "deafened with the noise of this new craze."[4] Abercius and his colleague had to work to create and maintain the Christian fellowship that stretched from Rome to Mesopotamia; they were engaged in the process of self-differentiation and identity creation.

When historians and theologians used to tell the story of Christianity's "crisis of Gnosticism," they would explain, as the title of one important article put it, "Why the Church Rejected Gnosticism."[5] (Strangely, at least one scholar has included even the New Prophecy in "Gnosticism.")[6] But as we have seen already in the previous chapter, there was no single "Church" that could accept or reject anything, nor was there a multiform heresy called "Gnosticism" to be accepted or rejected. There was a Gnostic school of thought, with its distinct interpretation of the Christian message, and there were a number of other Christian teachers and groups who disagreed with the Gnostics on particular points. But the dynamic of self-differentiation and boundary formation in which the Gnostics and their opponents participated was far more complex than simple "rejection" of one party by another. A variety of Christian groups negotiated their relationships with each other and with non-Christians as well. The goal of this chapter is to sketch some of the ways in which Christians of the second and third centuries responded to the Gnostics and to each other. We shall explore the strategies by which Christians presented themselves as having the true Christian message and others as teaching what is incomplete or false.

We have already seen some of these strategies as practiced both by the Gnostics and their rivals. The Gnostics, we saw in Chapter 3, made claims to authority and truth by composing their writings as revelations that came to authoritative figures of the distant and recent past (Adam, Nōrea, the apostle John). They used the genealogical narratives of Genesis to depict themselves as the spiritual heirs of Seth, the good son of Adam and Eve, and others as descendants of more ambivalent or evil figures, like Cain and the sons of Noah. Gnostic authors asserted that other readers of the Bible did not understand it because they failed to see that Moses mistakenly identified Ialdabaōth as the ultimate God; in contrast, the Gnostics had the revelatory insight to offer the true readings and to correct Moses' errors. In turn, we saw in Chapter 4 the strategies that Valentinus, Marcion, and Justin employed to label their opponents as false Christians and to legitimate their own teachings, including claims to apostolic succession and the notion of "heresy."

In this chapter, I look at four more representative movements or figures: the Valentinian School, Irenaeus of Lyons, Clement of Alexandria, and Origen. These Christians adapted and augmented the tactics that we have already seen as they reacted to the remarkable teachings of the Gnostic school of thought and others. Because I have taken the Gnostics as my starting point, so to speak, I follow a conversation that circled around the issues that they raised, especially the teaching of higher *gnōsis*, the use and interpretation of Scripture, and the multiplicity of God. If we were to focus on other strands of early Christian self-definition, such as the authority of the martyr or the problems of Church discipline, then we would need to examine a somewhat different cast of characters, one that included, for example, Bishop Cyprian of Carthage (d. 258), a contemporary of Origen. That story would be just as important for understanding the changing character of Christian groups in the second and third centuries and beyond.

The Gnostics, however, lead us primarily to Greek-speaking teachers of Christian thought. In Rome during the 140s and 150s, Justin, Valentinus, and Marcion were all teachers of Christianity who guided their own circles of students. They were not also what we would call ordained clergy, that is, bishops or presbyters. Bishops and presbyters were also teachers, but they more explicitly tied their teaching activity to the ritual life of the sacraments and a more formal institutional setting of worshiping communities. Christian leaders of the second and third centuries had to negotiate the relationship between teaching and the formal clergy, between teacher-centered study circles and more formally constituted Christian communities, and between what they considered true and false versions of Christianity.

## Teachers of an Apostolic Tradition: The Valentinian School

Valentinus's program of adapting the Gnostic myth and developing its more overtly Christian features continued in the work of a school of Christian theologians who looked to him for inspiration: the Valentinian school of thought. So successful was this movement that it rapidly eclipsed the Gnostics as the greater danger in the minds of opponents like Irenaeus. Unlike the Gnostics, who practiced a highly distinctive ritual of baptism and appear to have rejected the Eucharist, the Valentinians participated fully in the baptism and Eucharist of other Christians and may have had even more rituals of their own. Valentinian teachers presented their ideas as the correct interpretations of Christian scriptures and creeds, and they claimed apostolic authority for their message. Like the Gnostic school of thought and other philosophical schools in antiquity, Valentinian groups sought to facilitate the progress of their adherents in knowledge and virtue, that is, to teach them a way of life that would lead to salvation.[7] Valentinian theologians developed rich and compelling teachings on the entire range of subjects that Christian intellectuals usually considered—God, Christ, sin, and salvation, the sacraments, the nature of the Church, the resurrection, and so on—but here I shall focus on their strategies of self-differentiation with respect to other Christians. How did Valentinian Christians present their reinventions of Christianity as the true ones?

"Valentinianism" existed in a range of social forms and related to other Christian communities in diverse ways. On a minimal basis, it was a mode of Christian thought or a way of understanding the Christian message with which any educated Christian could engage without necessarily joining a group. There must have been bishops and presbyters in local communities whose preaching and teaching reflected Valentinian ideas without any awareness on their part or that of their congregants that these ideas were, as others might charge, suspect or out of "the mainstream." This situation might resemble a modern Christian congregation in which the minister's sermons and biblical interpretations might be heavily influenced by Karl Barth or by liberation theology. We know that in the 190s a Valentinian named Florinus served as a presbyter in the Roman Church under the non-Valentinian Bishop Victor. It is not clear whether people recognized Florinus as a Valentinian only on the basis of his views or because he also participated in an organized group of Valentinians. When early Valentinians became visible as a distinct community, it was usually because they formed study groups similar to other philosophical schools in antiquity. These groups operated alongside and as a supplement to other Christian communities: a Christian might worship weekly in a house church near his or her home but also participate in meetings of study and discussion led by a Valentinian teacher.

Valentinians incorporated their unique relationship to other Christians into their theology and reached out to them. For example, they borrowed terminology from Paul's First Letter to the Corinthians (2:14–15) and referred to themselves as "spiritual ones" *(pneumatikoi)* and to non-Valentinian Christians as merely "animate ones" *(psuchikoi)*. According to Irenaeus's account of Valentinian teachings, "animate" Christians would receive a lesser form of salvation at the end of time than the "spiritual ones" would—but salvation nonetheless. When the spirituals are restored to the fullness (the Valentinian version of the Gnostics' entirety), the animates will "gain repose" in a place outside of it.[8] The comprehensive Valentinian work *The Tripartite Tractate,* however, suggests that the distinction between "animates" and "spirituals" will be overcome in God's final act of reconciliation: "If, in fact, we confess the kingdom in Christ, it is for the abolishment of all diversity, inequality, and difference. For the end will regain the form of existence of a single one, just as the beginning was a single one."[9] Similarly, another Valentinian teacher called the final consummation a "wedding banquet, which is shared by all the saved, until all become equal and recognize one another."[10]

And indeed, Valentinians showed pastoral interest in their fellow Christians, often inviting them to join them for advanced study and thus eventually to become "spirituals" themselves. For example, a surviving letter from the Valentinian theologian Ptolemy introduces a non-Valentinian Christian named Flora to some basic Valentinian ideas (ethics, the lower status of the creator god) and then invites her to study further with him.[11] The anti-Valentinian Bishop Irenaeus complained bitterly that Valentinians use "persuasion and rhetoric" to "attract the simple to pursue the quest" for advanced knowledge of God and Christ.[12] The Valentinians presented themselves and their teachings as the deeper or higher meaning of whatever form of Christianity to which potential followers adhered. Their division of Christians into "animates" and "spirituals" functioned more like stages in one's progression into acquaintance than as rigid, pre-determined sets of people.[13]

Irenaeus lamented, too, that the Valentinians "speak like us but think differently."[14] That is, the Valentinians accepted the same scriptures and basic doctrines as Irenaeus, but interpreted them differently, often in what Irenaeus took to be a more metaphorical or symbolical fashion. For example, all Christians agreed that "Christ was raised from the dead" (Romans 6:4) and that Christians, too, would rise like him (1 Corinthians 15). In Irenaeus's view, this meant that Christ rose from the grave, body and soul, and so would Christians at the end of history: "We too must await the time of our resurrection fixed by God."[15] According to one Valentinian author, however, the Christian's resurrection is his or her gradual transcendence of the material world through contemplation of increasingly higher realities. Resurrection does not lie in the future but is available now: "Leave the state of dispersion and bondage," the author exhorts, "and then you already have resurrection."[16] A Valentinian could affirm with fellow Christians who were not Valentinians a shared belief in resurrection from the dead, but would have his or her own understanding of what that means—as indeed all Christians did. At this point no single understanding had emerged as normative. Still, the rhetoric of some Valentinian works suggests that their authors understood that they had to relate their views to other Christian ideas that may have been more widespread. For instance, Ptolemy complained that "many people" have misunderstood the Law of Moses, and another Valentinian teacher remarked that "few" comprehend the true meaning of resurrection.[17]

The Gnostics drew on the Bible for their teachings, but they did so often by rewriting biblical narratives, especially from Genesis, in order to correct their meaning. They seemed to create new scriptures for themselves (The Revelation of Adam, The Gospel of Judas) as much as they used texts that other Jews and Christians honored. The Reality of the Rulers appears to replace Genesis just as much as it interprets it. The

Valentinians, in contrast, did not create new scriptures; rather, they were pioneers in the close exegesis of Jewish and Christian scriptures and produced some of the earliest known commentaries on biblical books. The Valentinian thinker Heracleon wrote "notes" or "comments" (hupomnēmata) on the Gospel of John and perhaps on other gospels as well.[18] Like most other Christian teachers, Heracleon and his colleagues interpreted biblical texts allegorically or symbolically and so argued that Valentinian teachings were to be found in them. For example, in the fourth chapter of John, Jesus tells the Samaritan woman at the well that "the hour is coming when you will worship the Father neither on this mountain nor in Jerusalem" (John 4:21). Heracleon interprets this statement as symbolically teaching that "spiritual ones" (that is, Valentinians) worship neither created things as the pagans did ("mountain") nor the creator god of this world as the Jews and many other Christians did ("Jerusalem"), but the higher ultimate God.[19] Valentinian exegetes also made extensive use of Paul's letters in explicating their theologies.[20]

Indeed, Valentinian teachers frequently invoked the authority of Paul (and of the apostles in general) to legitimate their doctrines and their identity as teachers. As we saw in the previous chapter, Valentinian theologians asserted that Valentinus had studied with Theudas, a disciple of Paul. Followers of another Christian teacher, Basilides, an older contemporary of Valentinus, made a similar claim about their theological hero, but they traced his intellectual pedigree back to the apostle Peter through a certain Glaucias.[21] By tracing a similar lineage to Paul, the Valentinians professed a kind of apostolic succession for themselves: Paul had transmitted his teachings to Theudas, who passed them on to Valentinus, and now these teachings have come to the students of Valentinus (and their students in turn). Ptolemy suggested to Flora that she might be "deemed worthy of the apostolic tradition, which even we have received by succession . . . at least if, like good rich soil that has received fertile seeds, you bear fruit."[22] One Valentinian author wrote, "The father anointed the son; and the son anointed the apostles, and the apostles anointed us."[23] Another attributed a prayer for authority and enlightenment to "Paul the Apostle."[24] The claim to special connection with an apostle through a chain of successors functioned as a powerful bid for authority and recognition as having the most authentic Christian teaching. Ptolemy's hope that Flora would prove "worthy of the apostolic tradition" indicates that at least portions of this tradition were reserved for more advanced Christians.

Baptism and the Eucharist played important roles in Valentinian spirituality. Their references to baptism suggest that their understanding of Christian initiation contained the same elements one finds in baptism in other Christian groups: a period of instruction, one or more anointings with oil, exorcisms, immersion, laying on of hands.[25] Valentinians must have undergone initiation in ordinary congregations or practiced their own baptism, which nonetheless did not differ much if at all from that of other Christians. Whichever was the case, baptism could not be effective without the instruction and growth in knowledge and virtue that Valentinian teaching provided: "It is not the bath alone that liberates, but also the acquaintance: Who were we? What have we become? Where were we? Into what place have we been thrown? Where are we going? From what are we ransomed? What is generation? What is regeneration?"[26] Valentinian sources suggest that they may have observed some rituals that were specific to them. For example, one group of Valentinians may have developed their own ritual for death long before other Christians did.[27] Several sources mention a ritual called "bridal chamber." "Bridal chamber" appears to refer to the potential reunion of the human soul with its angelic counterpart or spiritual alter ego. Scholars disagree, however, about whether "bridal chamber" in fact refers to a distinct ritual or represents a Valentinian understanding of the meaning of baptism.[28]

The Valentinian movement, then, had a complex relationship with other Christian groups. It featured independent study circles that worked like philosophical schools and supplemented worship and participation in non-Valentinian house churches. And yet some house churches may have had clergy whose theology was Valentinian, even if the house church did not have a "Valentinian" identity. Valentinian teachers reflected this ambiguous position. They claimed special authority inherited from the apostle Paul, presented their teachings as the hidden or symbolic meanings of generally shared Jewish and Christian scriptures, and reflected on the differences between Valentinian or advanced Christians ("spiritual ones") and their non-Valentinian brothers and sisters or less advanced Christians ("animate ones"). Evidence suggests that during the third century and later, Valentinian Christianity increasingly took on the character of a fully independent network of churches, similar to that of the Marcionites. For example, in the late fourth century a Christian mob attacked a Valentinian worship building—a sign that Valentinians by this point were clearly distinct from other Christians.[29]

## Bishops and Presbyters, Not Teachers:
## Irenaeus of Lyons (ca. 155–ca. 202)

As we have seen repeatedly, Irenaeus was among the most prominent critics of the Gnostics, but he considered the Valentinians the greater threat to his own congregation. Their more overt Christian character and their pastoral interest in other Christians made them, to his mind, wolves in sheep's clothing (Matthew 7:15).[30] Irenaeus's Christian community in Lyons had endured a period of harsh persecution, in which it had lost its previous bishop. Irenaeus was eager to protect his depleted and fragile Church from what he saw as additional harm from false Christians. His work exemplifies several strategies for differentiating one's own community and beliefs from those of other Christians, including a claim to a more institutional and public apostolic succession, a two-fold Christian Bible interpreted through a "rule of faith," heresiology, and the role of the bishop.

In writing his magnum opus *Detection and Overthrow of Gnōsis Falsely So-Called,* Irenaeus took over Justin Martyr's heresiological model, which we examined in the last chapter. Irenaeus claimed that his work was even more effective against the Valentinians than that of his predecessors (*AH* 4.pref.2), and in fact his book proved so popular that Christian scribes stopped copying Justin's *Against All the Schools of Thought That Have Arisen,* which now appeared obsolete. Irenaeus elaborated on Justin's concept of a chain of heretical teachers and groups that originated in Simon Magus. Unlike Justin the independent philosopher, however, Irenaeus the bishop portrayed the episcopate as the holy counterpart to the demonic succession of heretics. True bishops, Irenaeus claimed, could trace their lineage back to (at least) one of the original apostles. As an example, he provided such a genealogy for the bishops of Rome, for that Church "is greatest, most ancient, and known to all" (*AH* 3.1–3). We should remember that it was the followers of Basilides and Valentinus, heretics in the eyes of Irenaeus, who pioneered this strategy of legitimation. Irenaeus adopted it, but with a polemical twist. While the Valentinians appear to have presented at least part of the apostolic tradition that they received as reserved for advanced Christians ("spiritual ones"), Irenaeus insisted that the tradition that the apostles transmitted through the bishops was fully public and accessible to all.

Irenaeus stressed this difference between a teaching given to all Christians and a secret or reserved tradition of more advanced teachings. If the apostles had any "secret teachings," he argued, they surely would have taught them to their successors, the bishops. In fact, however, the very notion of a more hidden apostolic tradition turned the apostles into hypocrites. His opponents "claim that the apostles hypocritically made their teaching according to the capacity of the hearers and gave answers according to the prejudices of the inquirers . . . Thus the Lord and the apostles expressed their teaching not truthfully but hypocritically, as each could hold it" (*AH* 3.3.1; 3.5.1). What the Gnostics and Valentinians would doubtless view as the normal pedagogy of a teacher (starting with basic concepts and moving toward more advanced ideas), Irenaeus condemned as hypocrisy. Instead, the bishop asserted, the true apostolic tradition is "manifest in the whole world" and "easy to receive from the Church" (*AH* 3.3.1; 3.4.1).

Like the Valentinians and Clement of Alexandria (to whom I shall turn next), Irenaeus thought of Christian authority in terms of teachers and a school. The apostles, he said, passed on to the bishops "their own position of teaching" (*AH* 3.3.1). For Irenaeus, however, this "position of teaching" consisted not simply of a set of doctrines or ideas; rather, it was an office, the bishop, and tied to an institution, the Church. Therefore, Irenaeus pointedly did not call bishops "teachers"; he reserved that term and its connotation of independence and suspicious originality for leaders of groups that he opposed. As Virginia Burrus writes, for Irenaeus, "heretics have teachers; the orthodox have bishops and presbyters. Heretics have free-floating, and hence mutable, doctrines; the orthodox preserve their tradition within an institutional context."[31]

In response to Gnostic retellings of the Septuagint and to Marcion's rejection of it, Irenaeus promoted an embryonic biblical canon, consisting of two parts, an Old and a New Testament, with four gospels. The Bible, Irenaeus said, contains two covenants. The first may be "old" and more suited for "slaves" and the "undisciplined," and the second may be "new" and meant for "children" and "free" people—but they come from the same God, who adjusted his revelation to the progression of humanity (*AH* 4.9). He accused various groups of relying too much on a single gospel; for example, the Valentinians used the Gospel of John excessively (he claimed). In fact, Christians must use all four gospels (Matthew, Mark, Luke, and John), and not others (*AH* 3.11.7–9). Like the

Valentinians, Irenaeus interpreted the Old Testament allegorically in order to find his own views in it—in his case, to demonstrate the unity of
the Old and New Testaments and the single identity of their God. He
argued that the Bible's overarching "plot line" or "project" *(hupothesis)*
was not the Gnostics' myth of cosmic devolution and return but the
story of the single God of Israel's relationship with humanity, summarized in a "rule of faith."[32] The rule anticipated and/or reflected creeds
that converts would learn when they became Christians:

> The Church, which is dispersed throughout the entire world and to the
> ends of the earth, received from the apostles and their disciples this faith in
> one God the Father Almighty, "who made heaven and earth and the sea
> and all that is in them" [Exodus 20:11], and in one Christ Jesus, the Son of
> God, incarnate for our salvation, and in the Holy Spirit, who predicted
> through the prophets the dispensations of God, the coming, the birth from
> the Virgin, the passion, the resurrection from the dead, and the ascension
> of the beloved Jesus Christ our Lord in the flesh into the heavens, and his
> coming from the heavens in the glory of the Father to "recapitulate all
> things" [Ephesians 1:10] and to raise up all flesh of the human race . . . and
> that he might execute a just judgment on all and send to eternal fire "the
> spiritual powers of wickedness" [Ephesians 6:12], the lying and apostate
> angels, and people who are impious, unjust, wicked, and blasphemous,
> while on the contrary he might give incorruptible life as a reward to the
> just and equitable who keep his commandments and persevere in his love,
> some from the beginning, others since their conversion, and surround
> them with eternal glory (*AH* 1.10.1).

Christ himself had delivered this rule to his apostles, who transmitted it
to the bishops who followed them; thus, the rule was the same throughout the one Church (*AH* 1.10; 3.2–4).

Irenaeus admitted that, in contrast to this clear rule, the Scriptures are
not always unambiguous; rather, some things are written "in parables."
The Christian exegete may "work out" the meaning of such passages as
long as he "conforms to the general scheme *(hupothesis)* of the faith"
(*AH* 1.10.3). In fact, given the slipperiness of the Scriptures (that is, that
Gnostics and Valentinians and Marcionites could all find their views
in them), it is no surprise that Irenaeus privileged the rule and the apostolic tradition over the Scriptures: Christians do just fine if they have
received the true faith handed down from the apostles through the bishops, but lack the Scriptures (*AH* 3.4.2). Irenaeus faced a multitude of

rival Christianities, not just the Gnostics, and emphasized the unity and consistency of the one Church in contrast to the multiplicity and diversity of his opponents. His narrative of a decline from an original period of unity and truth paralleled the Gnostic myth of a fall from an original spiritual unity. Justin's heresiological model of multiple heretical teachers originating in a single source (Simon Magus) facilitated this representation.

In Irenaeus's program, the bishop was responsible for enforcing with practical measures the truth that he received from the apostles. Differentiation from rival Christian groups was only one factor in the emergence of the bishop as the single leader of Christians in a city, but it was an important one. Bishop Victor of Rome (ca.189–199) may serve as one example of the Irenaean paradigm in action.[33] As we saw in the previous chapter, before Victor the diverse Christian groups in Rome usually tolerated one another and expressed their unity by sending tokens of the Eucharistic elements to one another. Victor at first acted within this tradition, recognizing representatives of the New Prophecy movement ("Montanism") as legitimate Christians and the Valentinian Florinus as one of his presbyters. The existence of multiple house churches hindered any simple bilateral division of "orthodox" from "others."[34] But Irenaeus wrote to the presbyter Florinus from Lyons and chastised him for teachings that were "inconsistent with the church": "The presbyters before us, those who went around especially with the apostles, did not transmit such teachings to you." Irenaeus understood that the Valentinian Florinus was not separate from the wider Christian community in Rome, for Irenaeus contrasted him with "heretics outside the church."[35] In turn, Irenaeus wrote to Bishop Victor and exhorted him to "expel" Florinus's writings as "blasphemy," particularly dangerous for Christians because Florinus could claim to be "one of you," that is, one of Victor's circle. It seems that Victor did fire Florinus, for the later Church historian Eusebius refers to him as "fallen from the presbytery of the church."[36] The Christian teacher Praxeas, recently arrived from Asia Minor, likewise urged the Roman bishop to withdraw fellowship from the adherents of the New Prophecy. Victor did this as well and cut off fellowship also with another Christian teacher, Theodotus, the shoemaker.[37] Because the bishop's authority was closely tied to the Eucharist over which he presided, the withdrawal of communion served him as a primary means of establishing boundaries between his own and rival Christian groups.

Irenaeus, however, did not try to eliminate every kind of diversity from the churches; in another exchange with Victor, he urged the Roman bishop to tolerate differences among Christians. In this case, Roman Christians who came from Asia Minor celebrated Easter and the fast that preceded it on a schedule different from that of other Christians in Rome, including Victor. Bishop Victor threatened to withdraw fellowship from Christians who followed the traditions of Asia Minor unless they conformed to his practice. Irenaeus, however, tried to dissuade Victor from this course of action. Recognizing that the Christians from Asia Minor were observing a tradition that dated back to the earliest years of Christianity, Irenaeus argued that it was customary to allow for "particular practice" in certain areas, concluding that "disagreement about the fast confirms agreement about the faith."[38] Irenaeus, then, valued conformity to the rule of faith more than uniformity in ritual practice, particularly when differences in practice enjoyed the precedent of the ancient tradition that he valued so highly.

Moreover, Irenaeus's own thought did not differ as fundamentally from the teachings of the Gnostics and the Valentinians as he would have liked his readers to think. We have noted already that Irenaeus was just as willing as his opponents were to interpret biblical passages allegorically to support his views; he just used a different overall myth as the framework for his exegetical decisions. Like all the Christians we have met so far, including the Gnostics, Irenaeus did not believe in simply one God. Rather, he distinguished between the ultimate God, the Father, who is "uncreated, beyond grasp, invisible," and two clearly lower manifestations of God: the Word or Son, who "establishes, that is, works bodily and consolidates being," and the Spirit, who "disposes and shapes the various powers."[39] Like the Gnostics' Invisible Spirit, Irenaeus's Father is "invisible and inaccessible to creatures," and thus "it is through the Son that those who are to approach God must have access to the Father."[40] Again, the Father cannot be measured and must be revealed only by the Son, who (unlike the Father) can be known (AH 4.20.1, 6). So, too, there are multiple other beings that exist between this divine triad and humanity: "The earth is encompassed by seven heavens, in which dwell Powers and Angels and Archangels, giving homage to the Almighty God who created all things." Irenaeus gives the names of the seven heavens, beginning with Wisdom, and continuing with Understanding, Counsel, Fortitude, Knowledge, Godliness, and Fear of the Spirit.[41] Certainly Irenaeus's divine realm and created cosmos were less elaborate and populated than those of the Gnostics or Valentinians, but he just as clearly belonged to the same intellectual milieu as they, one in which human knowledge of an inaccessible highest God required the mediation of multiple divine beings.

## The Teacher Is the Real Presbyter:
## Clement of Alexandria (ca. 160–215)

In Alexandria, Clement and Origen resembled Valentinian teachers in that they offered small groups of students the opportunity to advance spiritually in the study of Christian scriptures and doctrines, but each endeavored to differentiate himself from his competitors and to stake out some relationship to the emerging networks of episcopally led communities. Clement, for example, had to differentiate himself on at least two fronts. On the one hand, he portrayed his "domesticated *gnōsis*" (not Clement's term) as more faithful to original Christian doctrine than that offered by competing teachers like the Gnostics and Valentinians, whom he called heretics.[42] On the other hand, he defended his philosophical speculation and advanced instruction of true "Gnostics" against Christians whom he described as "those who are called orthodox" and who insisted on "the bare faith alone."[43]

Although Eusebius later assimilated him to church structures by portraying him as the head of a catechetical school formally tied to the episcopate, Clement more likely operated as a fully independent Christian teacher.[44] As we saw in Chapter 2, he challenged Gnostics and Valentinians at their own game by calling his ideal Christian "our Gnostic" or "the Gnostic, properly speaking" and referring to his competitors as "falsely named" Gnostics. He countered the Gnostic use of genealogical and racial language to define themselves through his own use of procreative and kinship metaphors to authorize his own teachings and to delegitimate those of his rivals.[45] Also like the Valentinians, Clement claimed to receive a special tradition of teaching from the apostles. Unlike Irenaeus, Clement did not trace this apostolic tradition through bishops, nor did he depict it as publicly available to any and all Christians. "*Gnōsis* itself," he argued, "has come down by succession to a few people, transmitted by the apostles in unwritten form" (*Str.* 6.7.61.3). Echoing Ptolemy the Valentinian by calling transmitted teachings "seeds," Clement claimed that his teachers "preserved the true tradition of the blessed doctrine in direct line from Peter, James, John, and Paul, the holy apostles, child inheriting from father . . . and came with God's help to plant in us those ancestral and apostolic seeds" (*Str.* 1.1.11.3).[46] Clement pointedly did not trace his academic lineage to a single apostle, but to four, and did not name the teachers who intervened between these apostles and himself, thereby portraying himself, in contrast to his Valentinian and other competitors, as possessing not a particular strain of Christian teaching, but the fullness of apostolic teaching, transmitted in an academic succession beyond scrutiny.[47]

Clement exhibited an attitude toward Christian communities led by bishops and presbyters that resembled that of the Valentinians in its ambivalent openness. Professing his adherence to the teachings of the wider Church, Clement nonetheless offered his students a form of secret knowledge passed down not through bishops but through his unnamed teachers (*Str.* 1.1.11–13). He made use of a range of sacred literature that belies the notion of a closed canon.[48] Moreover, that sacred literature was filled with what Clement (like Irenaeus) called "parables." The parabolic enigmas of the Scriptures, Clement said, are not accessible to everyone, but only to "the elect among human beings, those who have been chosen out of faith for *gnōsis*" (*Str.* 6.15.126.2). That is, just as the Valentinian teachers asserted that "animate" Christians could advance to become "spiritual" ones under their guidance, Clement could lead students from faith to *gnōsis* through their study of the Scriptures under his direction.

In turn, Clement very seldom referred to bishops or other clergy and their communities. He pointedly claimed that the person who "has lived perfectly and gnostically" is "really a presbyter of the church" even if "he has not been ordained by human beings" (*Str.* 6.13.106.1–2).[49] Clement's pamphlet *Who Is the Rich Man Who Is Being Saved?* explained how a wealthy Christian could achieve virtue and salvation without divesting himself of all his wealth (as Mark 10:17–31 seems to suggest). Clement encouraged the rich Christian to submit to "some man of God as a trainer and guide," that is, to follow a teacher such as Clement. He followed that exhortation with a cautionary tale in which a bishop failed to provide proper guidance to a spirited young man.[50] Clement's study circle provided the surest path to salvation and to spiritual perfection as a true Gnostic. Clement wrote at a time when Demetrius, the first single bishop of Alexandria, was emerging and claiming authority. Clement probably allied himself with Demetrius's worshiping community, but he never mentioned him in his works.

Still, Clement insisted on fidelity to the wider Christian community that he called the Church. The Church, he said, is the Mother of Christians, just as God is their Father.[51] Like Irenaeus, Clement argued that proper interpretation of the Scriptures is governed by what he called "the ecclesiastical norm *(kanōn)*" or "the norm of truth" *(Str.* 6.15.125.2–3; 7.16.94.5). Unlike Irenaeus, however, Clement does not identify this "norm" or "rule" with a creedal narrative of specific teachings, but with vaguer principles of comprehensiveness in the use of the Scriptures, adherence to the original teaching of Jesus, and not following one's own peculiar interests, intellectual or otherwise. Those who participate in heresies, he said, "adulterate the truth and steal the norm of the church by gratifying their own desires and vanity and by deceiving their neighbors" *(Str.* 7.16.105.5). Their "human assemblies" originated later than "the catholic church" *(Str.* 7.17.106.3). The Church is one, but the heresies are numerous, identified by the names of their founders (Valentinians) or their places of origin or whatever *(Str.* 7.17). His opponents, Clement said, do not teach "the mysteries of ecclesiastical *gnōsis*" *(Str.* 7.16.97.4). When he makes such claims, Clement sounds a great deal like Irenaeus.

As an independent teacher rather than a bishop, however, Clement occupied a more ambiguous position than Irenaeus. He shared the commitment to *gnōsis,* the higher and more immediate knowledge of God and what is truly real, which animated the Gnostic school of thought and the Valentinian school. Moral and intellectual training under a trustworthy teacher like Clement made such *gnōsis* possible, for he had received higher teachings from a succession of inspired teachers extending back to the apostles. And yet Clement differentiated himself from his Gnostic and Valentinian rivals, who offered that same kind of moral and intellectual guidance, in part by claiming his own greater fidelity to an allegedly more widely shared tradition. Clement presented himself as offering the advanced and esoteric gnosis that other teachers did, but one tied more closely to Christians like Irenaeus. Paul the Apostle, Clement argued, taught that "*gnōsis,* which is the perfection of faith, advances beyond catechesis, in accordance with the magnitude of the Lord's teaching and the ecclesiastical norm" *(Str.* 6.18.165.1). Clement offered that combination of adherence to "the ecclesiastic norm" and something more, something that reflected the "magnitude" of what Jesus really taught—"ecclesiastical *gnōsis.*"

Presbyter and Teacher:
Origen (ca. 185–ca. 251)

Origen clearly presented himself as a man of the Church and eventually joined the clergy, but he, too, placed a high value on the Christian's advancement in study and discipline. As a teacher of advanced Christian thought, Origen, like Clement, had to differentiate himself both from rival teachers of differing philosophical commitments and from the ordinary Christian assembly. On the one hand, Origen became the target of a bishop's attempt to control diversity and to consolidate authority. He articulated a model of authority that separated legitimate teaching from clerical office. On the other hand, he criticized "heretics" and promoted the Church's "rule" as a limit to biblical interpretation.

After the martyrdom of his father, the brilliant young Origen made his way into the salons of wealthy and intellectually inclined Christians in Alexandria, an environment dominated by "heretical" teachers, mainly Valentinians. Origen engaged these rivals in intellectual give-and-take but would not worship with them.[52] He worked, particularly in his *On First Principles,* to create a Christian "body" *(sōma)* of thought that could compete with those of the Gnostics and Valentinians.[53] It was his answer to the kind of comprehensive statements of Christian teaching that one finds in the Gnostics' *Secret Book According to John* or the Valentinians' *Tripartite Tractate.* Like Irenaeus, Origen relied on a rule of faith—"the teaching of the church, handed down in unbroken succession from the apostles"—to confront the "conflicting opinions" held by professed Christians. Irenaeus had stated that the rule gives Christian scholars some latitude in the interpretation of puzzling biblical passages, as long as they conform their readings to the rule. Origen took this principle further: he believed that the apostles deliberately left some teachings vague or unsubstantiated so that "lovers of wisdom," teachers like himself and his students, would have material with which to speculate and so "display the fruit of their ability" *(FP* pref.2–3). For Origen the rule functioned both as a limit to theological speculation and as a springboard or basis for it.

Like the Gnostic and Valentinian myths, Origen's Christian myth narrated a fall from an original state of spiritual unity into a material universe marred by evil, concluding with a return of all things to God. Origen, however, did not assign creation to an imperfect God, and he placed free will at the center of his narrative. In agreement with his

Gnostic and Valentinian rivals, Origen described the ultimate God as "incomprehensible and immeasurable," a "simple and wholly mental existence." So, too, like the Gnostics, Origen taught that "there is a certain affinity between the [human] mind and God, of whom the mind is an intellectual image, and that by reason of this fact the mind, especially if it is purified and separated from bodily matter, is able to have some perception of the divine nature" (FP 1.1.5–7). In other words, the human intellect is patterned after God, and we can gain acquaintance with God if we discipline our bodies and engage in study. We know God through his Son, the Word or Wisdom, whose relationship to the Father is "an eternal and everlasting begetting, as brightness is begotten from light." This "birth from the Father is as it were an act of his will proceeding from the mind." Origen insisted that the Son and, in turn, the Holy Spirit are not similar to the Gnostics' and Valentinians' "emanations," which "split the divine nature into parts . . . dividing God the Father" (FP 1.2.4, 6). Still, Origen's vocabulary for the generation of these divine persons—"begetting," "image"—echoed that of his rivals, even as his divine Trinity represented a much simpler multiform divinity.

So, too, for Origen, our bodies did not constitute our original and essential selves; rather, all created rational beings originated as minds, entities of pure reason alone. This was the past of every human being born on earth, as well as of angels, demons, and the heavenly creatures. These rational beings originally enjoyed unity with each other and God through contemplation of the Word, but they all fell away from love of God and unity with him by their own free turning away. They cooled in their affection for God to varying degrees. The diverse bodies that they now have, ranging from the bright and ethereal to the dull and the heavy, reflect the distance that they declined from God and are suited to each being's particular need for moral reformation. Our bodies, then, are, as the Gnostics imagined, additions to our immaterial selves and the result of a fall, but they do not, as the Gnostics thought, enslave us to cosmic forces but provide us with an opportunity for education in virtue. We learn to be virtuous by learning to control our bodies, which exacerbate our vulnerability to passions such as lust and anger. Our bodies' resurrection and eventual transformation will reflect our moral and intellectual progress, and in fact all rational beings will recover the lost original unity with God and each other. The mind returns to God through its own free will, guided by God's pedagogy of love and chastisement.[54] In its general plot and many of its central themes—fall, recovery, and contemplation—Origen's myth represented a brilliant adaptation of the earlier Christian myths that he denounced as heretical.

Just as *First Principles* resembled a Valentinian treatise like *Tripartite Tractate*, Origen more often presented his views in another way that his Valentinian rivals did—in scriptural commentaries filled with allegorical exegesis. In his *Commentary on John*, Origen quoted and refuted interpretations that the Valentinian teacher Heracleon had offered in his own similar work, and it is possible that Origen's use of the commentary genre reflected the influence of Heracleon and others. Origen did not dismiss Heracleon's readings out of hand; he could praise one of Heracleon's cleverer interpretations as "very powerful and ingenious."[55] But Origen much more often rebuked him for disparaging the Old Testament and its God, for proffering interpretations that did not appear substantiated by the wording of the text, for failing to consult passages from other biblical books to clarify the possible references of words and phrases in John, and for introducing doctrines that conflicted with the Church's "rule."[56] For example, he criticized Heracleon's interpretation of John 4:21, which we noted earlier, for violating "the rule followed by the majority in the church."[57] Other allegorical readers he criticized for simple lack of expertise: they were "unable to define precisely a simple ambiguity."[58] Of course, not reading the Bible allegorically could be equally dangerous. Elsewhere Origen condemned Jews and Christian "heretics" who did not read the Old Testament "according to the spiritual meaning but according to the bare letter" and so reached unacceptable theological conclusions. For example, Marcion mistakenly interpreted the God of the Old Testament to be literally as anger-filled as he appears and thus erroneously concluded that he was not the Father of Jesus Christ (*FP* 4.2.2). But in the case of allegorists such as Heracleon, the primary contrast Origen drew between himself and "heretical" readers was his adherence to the Church's rule; without such adherence, an exegete such as Heracleon simply interpreted incorrectly.

Clement had worked as an independent teacher, professing loyalty to a wider Church whose leadership seldom appeared in his works, but Origen's relationship to worshipping communities of Christians became both more formal and more complex. Origen's early interactions with rival Valentinian teachers indicates the diversity of Alexandrian Christianity, but during the same period that Bishop Victor was taking measures against "heretics" in Rome, Bishop Demetrius began to emerge as a strong leader in Alexandria. It seems that Demetrius at first welcomed the young Origen's efforts to refute Valentinians and others and to offer an alternative Christian education to theirs; the bishop endorsed Origen's school as an appropriate setting for new Christians to learn about the faith. But Demetrius's efforts to consolidate the bishop's authority to enforce doctrine and practice in the city eventually brought him into conflict with Origen's more speculative and free spirit. Origen did not restrict his teaching to elementary instruction for new converts, as Demetrius envisioned, but he organized the school with two levels, including an advanced tier for students who pursued the same kind of higher knowledge that Clement had taught. Origen's fame brought him invitations to lecture in foreign locations, and during one trip to Palestine, the bishop of Caesarea Maritima ordained him a presbyter. This action, along with a rumor that during a lecture in Athens Origen stated that the devil would be saved, led Demetrius around 230 to convene a group of bishops and have him expelled from the Church in Alexandria. Origen then relocated to Caesarea, where he set up a new school and preached as a presbyter.[59]

As a teacher and a preacher, Origen sought to address a variety of constituencies, ranging from ordinary churchgoers who could not read, to the educated (and not so educated) bishops who sought his theological expertise, to the aristocratic patrons who paid for his library and teams of scribes. He did not hesitate to use his learning and eloquence to aid bishops in combating "heresies"; at least twice, synods of bishops invited Origen to interrogate a fellow bishop suspected of heretical ideas.[60] In the wake of his conflict with Demetrius and enjoying the support of the bishop in Caesarea, Origen articulated a model of authority akin to those of Valentinus and Clement: the ideal Christian leader received the gift *(charisma)* of insight into the higher meaning of the Scriptures. Origen agreed with Clement that ordination as a bishop or presbyter did not coincide with teaching authority. He observed that the spiritually gifted person, the real bishop, was not always the visible bishop. The true priests, he said, are "those who are really dedicated to the divine word and to the worship of God."[61] Unlike Clement, however, Origen did not invoke a succession of teachers going back to the apostles as the conduit of either secret doctrines or intellectual authority. Instead, just as Valentinus seemed to suggest, the gift of insight came directly to the individual from God and bore fruit in the scholar's moral purity and exegetical labors. Origen certainly believed in esoteric or higher teachings that were available only to more advanced Christians, but gifted scholars derived these teachings directly from the Bible. Still, as a presbyter Origen found a place in the Church of Caesarea and was able to bring into or alongside the episcopally led community a conception of charismatic authority that challenged claims based solely on office. The bishop has grave responsibilities, Origen recognized, but the true leadership of the Church consists of the spiritual elite who interpret the Scriptures and convey their message of salvation to others.[62]

## From Strategies of Self-Differentiation to
## Establishing and Enforcing Orthodoxy

When the colleague of Abercius confronted the New Prophecy among the Christians in Galatia, he "spoke out for days on end in the church about these matters, and replied to every argument that they put forward." This Christian teacher's refutation of the teachings of New Prophecy so impressed the local presbyters that they asked him to leave with them a written summary of what he had said. He could not do so then, but the treatise that he dedicated to Abercius belatedly fulfilled their request.[63] For presbyters seeking to establish unity and conformity in their communities, a good teacher and well-made arguments were valuable things.

As they sought to invent and reinvent Christianity in the second and third centuries, Christian leaders tried to sort out what proper teaching was and who did it. In response to Gnostic pseudepigraphy, genealogical rhetoric, and theological claims, they developed a repertoire of strategies of self-differentiation: (1) modes of personalized teaching authority, expressed in claims either to visionary insight or to a succession of teachers or bishops, sometimes articulated in procreative or agricultural metaphors; (2) embryonic canons of the Bible, usually consisting of Old and New Testaments; (3) allegorical methods of scriptural reading, which articulated the unity of the bipartite Bible and enabled the elaboration of speculative ideas; (4) formulation of a "rule" of truth or faith as a limit to and/or inspiration for such reading and speculation; (5) heresiology as a means of trivializing a range of opponents and bolstering one's own claim to single and original truth; (6) withdrawal of communion. It is important to notice that not only Christians that scholars call "proto-orthodox" deployed these strategies; so did the so-called "losers" in the "battle for orthodoxy." The claims of Basilides and Valentinus to apostolic succession preceded those of Irenaeus. It may have been Marcion who withdrew from communion with his fellow Christians in Rome.

It is difficult to measure the success of such strategies in the pre-Constantinian era. Scholars have no reliable statistics for the numbers of Christians in different groups, and ancient authors can claim that "heretics" are numerous or few, depending on the hortatory point that they wish to make. It is telling, however, that Gnostic works that we know come from the third century (Zōstrianos, The Foreigner, Marsanes) are in conversation less with the Septuagint and distinctively Christian themes and more with contemporary Platonist discussions, and indeed it is in the context of competition with Plotinus's circle that we hear of them around 250.[64] By this time the lines between "Christianity," "Judaism," and traditional modes of philosophy and worship had become clearer, thanks to factors that were both internal and external. Internally, as we have seen, increasing diversity among Christians encouraged sharper definitions of what it meant to be a "true" Christian. Externally, persecution by the Roman government forced the issue of who was really a Christian rather than a Jew or a follower of other traditional religions. The myths taught by Valentinian theologians and by Origen retained some of the most compelling features of the Gnostic myth in much more explicitly Christian packages. The Gnostics had probably lost a lot of ground to these alternative modes of Christian gnōsis long before the conversion of Constantine.

And yet the multilateral efforts at self-differentiation in which the Gnostics and other groups played a prominent role did not produce a single "proto-orthodox" mode of piety or spiritual formation, but a variety of such. As much as an Irenaeus and an Origen shared, the striking differences in their theological visions and conceptions of authority complicate any attempt to place them on one side of any binary picture of the "proto-orthodox" arrayed against the Gnostics, the Valentinians, and so on. If the construction of a "Gnosticism" obscured the characters of the persons and groups assigned to it, likewise the category "proto-orthodox" can homogenize and so distort the diversity of pre-Constantinian Christianity. That diversity persisted into the fourth century and later, at times suppressed through anti-heretical measures but at times supported through, for example, the eventual embrace of monasticism. Although Irenaeus and others hoped to eliminate diversity and establish a single Church with a single truth, their efforts in fact contributed to the rich multiplicity of the imperial Christian culture that emerged in late antiquity.

The strategies that Irenaeus and other bishops employed did succeed, however, in creating boundaries, networks, and precedents that laid the basis for the universal or "catholic" Church that the bishops and Roman emperors after Constantine sought to create. During the second and third centuries, the practice of having a single bishop to oversee all the churches in a city (the monarchical episcopate) spread throughout the empire, in part to ensure unity and uniformity within and between Christian communities. Bishops, we have seen, portrayed themselves as guarantors of the sole tradition of proper belief and practice (the "rule of faith"), which they claimed was endangered by the speculations of independent philosophers or teachers (persons like Clement of Alexandria or Origen). Such speculations, they feared, could lead to such outright "heresies" as the Gnostic sect and the Valentinian school. Often drawn from the elite strata of society, bishops began to function in ways similar to patrons in Roman society. They dispensed spiritual benefits to ordinary believers through the sacraments and material benefits through a welfare system. In turn, they represented their followers before God and at times before earthly governors. The withdrawal of such benefits, excommunication, was the ultimate punishment available to the bishop in his effort to control deviance within his community. Such deviance, the bishop knew, would offend the divine Judge when he and his flock stood before him.[65]

Christians began to believe that unity and uniformity not only should characterize each individual congregation but also should prevail between congregations, as was fitting of a religion that claimed to be "universal" (in Greek, *katholikos*). Some individual bishops, especially of major Christian centers, claimed the authority to correct other bishops on their own. Drawing on the apostolic example of the Jerusalem meeting that I discussed in Chapter 4, bishops controlled diversity among themselves collectively through regional meetings ("councils" or "synods"). At these meetings a bishop of questionable orthodoxy might be publicly interrogated by a learned theologian, not always a bishop, and brought thereby to see the errors of his way of thinking. Such was the case when Bishop Beryllus of Bostra denied that Christ existed as a divine being before he became incarnate in Jesus. A synod of bishops summoned Origen and other theologians to question Beryllus, who came to see the error of his ways.[66] But in the case of a stubborn defendant, the gathered bishops could expel him and name a replacement in his see. When the bishop of Antioch, Paul of Samosata, refused to give up possession of the church buildings after a synod deposed him, Christians petitioned the Emperor Aurelian, who ordered that the civil authorities forcibly transfer control of the buildings to the Christians who were in communion with the bishops in Rome and Italy.[67] If councils of bishops in different regions disagreed on a major issue, as did bishops in North Africa and Italy on rebaptism of schismatics in the 250s, it was not clear how such a difference ought to be resolved, although participants believed it should be.

Constantine, then, when he became an engaged supporter of Christianity in 312, inherited both an ancient Roman tradition of suppressing offensive religious practices to ensure a good relationship with the divine and a more recent Christian tradition of controlling diversity through the episcopate and its councils. Constantine himself appears to have been comfortable with a vague and inclusive monotheism to which Christians and "pagans" (and Jews?) could adhere. When Christians engaged in an international dispute over the Alexandrian Arius's teaching about the divine status of the Word, Constantine expressed exasperation that they quarreled about such "small and utterly trivial" matters.[68] Such was not the attitude of the newly empowered bishops, and the emperor soon found himself involved in limiting Christian diversity. For example, when he wished to bestow imperial patronage on the Christians of North Africa and to grant exemptions from costly civic offices to their clergy, he had to choose between two rival Churches, the Donatists and the Caecilianists. He opted for the latter on the basis that they were in communion with the bishops in Rome and Italy.[69] This direction of imperial patronage and clerical exemptions to one group or another fostered conformity across geographical regions.

Constantine sponsored and enforced the decisions of the Council of Nicaea in 325. This meeting represented a significant advance in establishing and enforcing an international orthodoxy. As an explicitly (if not actually) "ecumenical" (worldwide) council, it claimed an authority superior to that of more regional councils, which had differed on the orthodoxy of Arius and his supporters. The emperor paid for the meeting and presided at its opening.[70] The results included the adoption of a creed, a successor to the rules promoted by Irenaeus, Origen, and others, to which clergy were required to subscribe. The full extent of Constantine's involvement in the bishops' deliberations is a matter of dispute, but he enforced the council's decisions by sending into exile those bishops who refused to comply. In accord with the long-standing Christian antipathy to internal diversity, the first objects of state religious control after Constantine were "heretics." Exile was the primary coercive measure available to emperors after Constantine, but by the turn of the fifth century heretics also faced imprisonment, heavy fines, and the confiscation of their places of worship.[71]

These measures to create a single orthodox Church in the fourth and later centuries were, as I have said, never entirely successful. Diversity and conflict characterized Christianity throughout the late ancient period—and beyond. Nonetheless, the attempt to create and maintain orthodoxy did not emerge as an entirely new project with the conversion of Constantine. Rather, bishops like Irenaeus and teachers like Origen laid the basis for it in their struggles with Gnostics, Valentinians, Marcionites, and others whom they considered false Christians. There may not have been a "Church" or a "Gnosticism" in the second century, when we have been told "the Church rejected Gnosticism." But the strategies of self-differentiation that bishops, Gnostics, and others employed as they sought to legitimate their own teachings and refute those of rivals helped to create the idea of a single Christianity and the eclipse of alternatives like that of *The Gospel of Judas*.

So did the Gnostics lose the horse race or battle in ancient Christianity after all? Or might we more charitably say that, simply in sociological terms, their attempt to invent Christianity resulted in a "failed" religious movement? As one scholar pointedly remarks, "If Christians today sing 'How Great Thou Art,' most do not have in mind the Great Seth."[72] Indeed, except for a small revival movement in the late twentieth century, medieval and modern Christians have been neither Gnostics nor Valentinians nor Marcionites. But neither, we must recognize, have they really been Irenaeans or Justinians or Origenists. No forms of Christianity that existed in the second and third centuries have survived intact today; rather, they have all contributed, in greater and lesser ways, to the ongoing development of Christianities. Traces of Gnostic thought and practice persisted in transformed modes. For example, the Gnostics' audacious creation of a comprehensive narrative of salvation from God through creation to Israelite history to Jesus and to the End provided an example that Christian theologians have followed down to the present day. Their interest in and strategies against malevolent demonic forces persisted in several Christian thinkers and became central in many forms of Christian monasticism. And their thoughtful discussions of how to gain mystical acquaintance with the God that cannot be known or described contributed to the thought of Plotinus and, through him, to later Christian mystics. The "Church" did not reject "Gnosticism," nor did the Gnostics "lose" to "proto-orthodoxy." Rather, the Gnostic school of thought, as small and limited as it was, played an important role in the process by which Christians, even today, continually reinvent themselves, their ideas, and their communities in light of their experience of Jesus Christ.

NOTES

SELECTED BIBLIOGRAPHY OF
PRIMARY SOURCES IN TRANSLATION

INDEX

# NOTES

## 1. Imagining "Gnosticism" and Early Christianities

1. Bart D. Ehrman, "Christianity Turned on Its Head: The Alternative Vision of the *Gospel of Judas,*" in Rodolphe Kasser, Marvin Meyer, and Gregor Wurst, eds., *The Gospel of Judas* (Washington: National Geographic Society, 2006), 77–120.

2. Tertullian, *Prescription Against the Heretics* 34–35.

3. Walter Bauer, *Orthodoxy and Heresy in Earliest Christianity* (1934) (Philadelphia: Fortress, 1971).

4. Colin H. Roberts, *Manuscript, Society, and Belief in Early Christian Egypt* (London: Oxford University Press, 1977).

5. Philip Rousseau, *Pachomius: The Making of a Community in Fourth-Century Egypt,* The Transformation of the Classical Heritage (Berkeley: University of California Press, 1985), 19.

6. Bart Ehrman, *Lost Christianities: The Battles for Scripture and the Faiths We Never Knew* (New York: Oxford University Press, 2003).

7. Karen L. King, *What Is Gnosticism?* (Cambridge: Harvard University Press, 2003), 71–148.

8. Robert Ford Campany, "On the Very Idea of Religions (in the Modern West and in Early Medieval China)," *History of Religions* 42 (2003): 287–319, at 317.

9. Irenaeus, *Proof of the Apostolic Preaching* 9, 20–21.

10. Karen L. King, "Which Early Christianity?" in Susan Ashbrook Harvey and David G. Hunter, eds., *The Oxford Handbook of Early Christian Studies* (Oxford: Oxford University Press, 2008), 66–84, at 73.

11. Campany, "On the Very Idea of Religions," 317.

12. My thinking about hybridity owes most to Homi K. Bhabha, *The Location of Culture* (London: Routledge, 1994), and (for its specific application to

religion) Kathryn Tanner, *Theories of Culture: A New Agenda for Theology*, Guides to Theological Inquiry (Minneapolis: Fortress, 1997).

13. Peter L. Berger, *The Sacred Canopy: Elements of a Sociological Theory of Religion* (Garden City, N.Y.: Doubleday, 1967); Clifford Geertz, *The Interpretation of Cultures: Selected Essays* (New York: Basic Books, 1973).

14. See Campany, "On the Very Idea of Religions," 318–319.

15. Rebecca Lyman, "Hellenism and Heresy," *Journal of Early Christian Studies* 11 (2003): 209–222.

16. Campany, "On the Very idea of Religions," 317.

17. Alain Le Boulluec, *Le Notion d'hérésie dans la literature grecque II$^c$–III$^c$ siècles* (Paris: Études augustiniennes, 1985).

18. Denise Kimber Buell, *Why This New Race: Ethnic Reasoning in Early Christianity* (New York: Columbia University Press, 2005).

19. Benjamin H. Dunning, *Aliens and Sojourners: Self as Other in Early Christianity*, Divinations: Rereading Late Ancient Religion (Philadelphia: University of Pennsylvania Press, 2009).

20. See, e.g., Paula Fredriksen, *Augustine and the Jews: A Christian Defense of Jews and Judaism* (New York: Doubleday, 2008), 6–10.

21. Tanner, *Theories of Culture*, 58, but not writing about the study of ancient Christianity.

22. Karen L. King, *The Secret Revelation of John* (Cambridge: Harvard University Press, 2006).

23. The author of the Acts of the Apostles says that the followers of Jesus were first called Christians in Antioch while Saul (Paul) was teaching there (Acts 11:26). But this claim is difficult to square with Paul's own letters.

24. For an important recent critique of key concepts and categories in early Christian studies, see Paula Fredriksen, "Mandatory Retirement: Ideas in the Study of Christian Origins Whose Time Has Come to Go," *Studies in Religion/ Sciences Religieuses* 35 (2006): 231–246.

25. King, "Which Early Christianity?" 74–80.

26. Ibid., 80.

27. Excellent accounts may be found in King, *What Is Gnosticism?* and Antti Marjanen, "What Is Gnosticism? From the Pastorals to Rudolph," in Antti Marjanen, ed., *Was There a Gnostic Religion?* Publications of the Finnish Exegetical Society 87 (Helsinki: Finnish Exegetical Society; Göttingen: Vandenhoeck & Ruprecht, 2005), 1-53.

28. Ugo Bianchi, ed., *Le Origini dello Gnosticismo: Colloquio di Messina, 13–18 Aprile 1966* (Leiden: Brill, 1967), xxvi–xxix.

29. Kurt Rudolph, *Gnosis: The Nature and History of Gnosticism* (San Francisco: Harper & Row, 1983), 2.

30. Michael Allen Williams, *Rethinking "Gnosticism": An Argument for Dismantling a Dubious Category* (Princeton: Princeton University Press, 1996).

31. Ibid., 51.

32. King, *What Is Gnosticism?* 218.

33. Ibid., 246.

34. For outstanding examples of such, see her *Secret Revelation of John* and *The Gospel of Mary of Magdala: Jesus and the First Woman Apostle* (Santa Rosa, Calif.: Polebridge, 2003).

35. Christoph Markschies, *Gnosis: An Introduction,* trans. John Bowden (London: T & T Clark, 2003), 15–17.

36. Antti Marjanen, "'Gnosticism,'" in Harvey and Hunter, eds., *Oxford Handbook of Early Christian Studies,* 203–220, at 210–211.

37. Marvin Meyer, *The Gnostic Discoveries: The Impact of the Nag Hammadi Library* (New York: HarperCollins, 2005), 42.

38. Meyer, *Gnostic Discoveries,* 61; Marjanen, "Gnosticism," 211.

39. Birger A. Pearson, *Gnosticism and Christianity in Roman and Coptic Egypt,* Studies in Antiquity & Christianity (London: T & T Clark, 2004), 201–223. In this paragraph and the next, this work is cited parenthetically in the text.

## 2. Identifying the Gnostics and Their Literature

1. Morton Smith, "The History of the Term Gnostikos," in Bentley Layton, ed., *The Rediscovery of Gnosticism: Proceedings of the International Conference on Gnosticism at Yale, New Haven, Connecticut, March 28–31, 1978,* vol. 2, *Sethian Gnosticism,* Studies in the History of Religions 41 (Leiden: Brill, 1981), 796–807; Bentley Layton, "Prolegomena to the Study of Ancient Gnosticism," in L. Michael White and O. Larry Yarbrough, eds., *The Social World of the First Christians: Essays in Honor of Wayne A. Meeks* (Minneapolis: Fortress, 1995), 334–350.

2. Bentley Layton, *The Gnostic Scriptures: A New Translation with Annotations and Introductions* (Garden City, N.Y.: Doubleday, 1987), 8.

3. *1 Clement* 36:2; 48:5; see also 40:1; 41:4.

4. *Barnabas* 19:1; see also 5:4; 9:8.

5. Irenaeus's use of the term *gnōstikos* has been the subject of extended scholarly debate. Some key discussions are Norbert Brox, "*Gnostikoi* als häresiologischer Terminus," *Zeitschrift für die neutestamentliche Wissenschaft und die Kunde der älteren Kirche* 57 (1966): 105–114; Adelin Rousseau and Louis Doutreleau, eds., *Irénée de Lyons, Contre les heresies,* Sources chrétiennes 100, 152–153, 210–211, 263–264, 293–294 (Paris: Éditions du Cerf, 1952–1982), vol. 294, pp. 350–354; M. J. Edwards, "Gnostics and Valentinians in the Church Fathers," *Journal of Theological Studies,* n.s. 40 (1989): 26–47, at 26–30; Michael Allen Williams, *Rethinking "Gnosticism": An Argument for Dismantling a Dubious Category* (Princeton: Princeton University Press, 1996), 33–37.

6. Irenaeus, *Against Heresies* 1.11.1. Henceforth I will cite this work as *AH* parenthetically in the text.

7. Tertullian, *Scorpiace* 1; *On the Soul* 18.

8. Tertullian, *Against the Valentinians* 39. An important modern scholar agrees with Tertullian on this point: Simone Pétrement, *A Separate God: The Christian Origins of Gnosticism,* trans. Carol Harrison (San Francisco: HarperCollins, 1990).

9. Clement of Alexandria, *Stromateis* 7.16.104.

10. Ibid., 1.13.58.2; 4.4.17.4.

11. Ibid., 3.4.30.1.

12. Tertullian, *Against Praxeas* 3; *Scorpiace* 15.

13. Porphyry, *Life of Plotinus* 16.

14. Hans-Martin Schenke, "Das sethianische System nach Nag-Hammadi-Handschriften," in Peter Nagel, ed., *Studia Coptica,* Berliner byzantinistischer Arbeiten 45 (Berlin: Akademie, 1974), 165–173, and "The Phenomenon and Significance of Gnostic Sethianism," in Layton, ed., *Rediscovery of Gnosticism,* vol. 2, *Sethian Gnosticism,* 588–616.

15. Layton, "Prolegomena."

16. Frederik Wisse, "Stalking Those Elusive Sethians," in Layton, ed., *Rediscovery of Gnosticism,* vol. 2, *Sethian Gnosticism,* 563–576.

17. Williams, *Rethinking "Gnosticism,"* 235–262.

18. Bentley Layton, "The Riddle of the Thunder (NHC VI,2): The Function of Paradox in a Gnostic Text from Nag Hammadi," in C. W. Hedrick and R. Hodgson Jr., eds., *Nag Hammadi, Gnosticism, and Early Christianity* (Peabody, Mass.: Hendrickson, 1986), 37–54; Paul-Hubert Poirier, "Introduction to *Thunder,*" in Marvin Meyer, ed., *The Nag Hammadi Scriptures: The International Version* (New York: HarperOne, 2007), 367–371.

19. David Brakke, "The Body as/at the Boundary of Gnosis," *Journal of Early Christian Studies* 17 (2009): 195–214.

20. M. J. Edwards, "Neglected Texts in the Study of Gnosticism," *Journal of Theological Studies,* n.s. 41 (1990): 26–50.

21. Alastair H. B. Logan, *The Gnostics: Identifying an Early Christian Cult* (London: T & T Clark, 2006).

22. Tuomas Rasimus, *Paradise Reconsidered in Gnostic Mythmaking: Rethinking Sethianism in Light of the Ophite Evidence,* Nag Hammadi and Manichaean Studies 68 (Leiden: Brill, 2009), esp. 54–61.

23. For a detailed examination of how *Judas* fits with other Gnostic works, see John D. Turner, "The Place of the *Gospel of Judas* in Sethian Tradition," in Madeliene Scopello, ed., *The "Gospel of Judas" in Context: Proceedings of the First International Conference on the "Gospel of Judas," Paris, Sorbonne, October 27th–28th, 2006,* Nag Hammadi and Manichaean Studies 62 (Leiden: Brill, 2008), 187–237. For the opposing view, see James M. Robinson, "The *Gospel of Judas* and the Sethians," *Coptica* 5 (2006): 50–68.

24. Heinrich von Staden, "Hairesis and Heresy: The Case of the *haireseis iatrikai*," in B. F. Meyer and E. P. Sanders, eds., *Jewish and Christian Self-Definition*, vol. 3, *Self-Definition in the Greco-Roman World* (Philadelphia: Fortress, 1982), 76–100, at 79–80.

25. Epiphanius of Salamis, *Against Heresies* 25–26, 39–40 (in Layton, *Gnostic Scriptures*, 185–214).

26. David Frankfurter, *Evil Incarnate: Rumors of Demonic Conspiracy and Satanic Abuse in History* (Princeton: Princeton University Press, 2006), 73–128.

27. Williams, *Rethinking "Gnosticism"*; "Sethianism," in Antti Marjanen and Petri Luomanen, eds., *A Companion to Second-Century Christian "Heretics,"* Supplements to *Vigiliae Christianae* 76 (Leiden: Brill, 2005), 32–63.

28. Karen L. King, *What Is Gnosticism?* (Cambridge: Harvard University Press, 2003), 158–162.

29. Karen L. King, *The Secret Revelation of John* (Cambridge: Harvard University Press, 2006), 100, 150–152.

30. For both objections, see Michael Allen Williams, "Was There a Gnostic Religion?" in Antti Marjanen, ed., *Was There a Gnostic Religion?* Publications of the Finnish Exegetical Society 87 (Helsinki: Finnish Exegetical Society; Göttingen: Vandenhoeck & Ruprecht, 2005), 55–79, at 75–76.

31. Layton, "Prolegomena," 344.

32. Pearson, "Gnosticism as a Religion," in Marjanen, ed., *Was There a Gnostic Religion?* 81–101, at 94.

33. Hippolytus, *The Refutation of All Heresies* 5.2; 5.6.4; 5.8.29; 5.11.1.

34. Ibid., 5.6.3–4.

35. Ibid., 5.9.22; 5.8.29.

36. Ibid., 5.23.3.

37. *The Books of Jeu and the Untitled Text in the Bruce Codex,* ed. Carl Schmidt, trans. Valerie MacDermot, Nag Hammadi Studies 13 (Leiden: Brill, 1978).

## 3. The Myth and Rituals of the Gnostic School of Thought

1. Pierre Hadot, *What Is Ancient Philosophy?* (Cambridge: Harvard University Press, 2002).

2. The origin of the name Barbēlō is obscure, but it might derive from Egyptian words for "emission" and "great"—thus, "the great emission" (Bentley Layton, *The Gnostic Scriptures: A New Translation with Annotations and Introductions* [Garden City, N.Y.: Doubleday, 1987], 15).

3. See the chart in John D. Turner, "Introduction to *The Holy Book of the Great Invisible Spirit*," in Marvin Meyer, ed., *The Nag Hammadi Scriptures: The International Edition* (New York: HarperOne, 2007), 248.

4. Williams, *Rethinking "Gnosticism": An Argument for Dismantling a Dubious Category* (Princeton: Princeton University Press, 1996), 155.

5. *First Thought* 39:13–40:4. The translation of this section of text is difficult, and thus scholarly interpretations differ.

6. See especially Plato, *Parmenides* 141–142.

7. Philo, *De Abrahamo* 119–122.

8. Philo, *Quis rerum divinarum heres?* 205.

9. Justin Martyr, *Second Apology* 6.

10. Justin Martyr, *Dialogue with Trypho* 55.1; *First Apology* 5.4; 46.2–5; 59.5; 63; 64.5; *Second Apology* 5.3.

11. Justin Martyr, *Dialogue with Trypho* 56.11.

12. Numenius, *On the Good* 5–6, fragments 16, 17, 20.

13. Alcinous, *Handbook of Platonism* 9.1.

14. Ibid., 10.2–4.

15. Ibid., 15.1.

16. Paula Fredriksen, "Mandatory Retirement: Ideas in the Study of Christian Origins Whose Time Has Come to Go," *Studies in Religion/Sciences Religieuses* 35 (2006): 231–246, at 241–243.

17. See John Dillon, "Monotheism in the Gnostic Tradition," in Polymnia Athanassiadi and Michael Frede, eds., *Pagan Monotheism in Late Antiquity* (Oxford: Oxford University Press, 1999), 69–79.

18. See Karen L. King, *The Secret Revelation of John* (Cambridge: Harvard University Press, 2006), 222–223, for parallels between the *Secret Book*'s account of the entirety and Genesis 1–3.

19. Symbolic interpretation: Origen, *On First Principles* 4.2. "Presence" or "word": *Targum Pseudo-Jonathan: Genesis,* trans. Michael Maher, The Aramaic Bible 1B (Collegeville, Minn.: Liturgical Press, 1992).

20. For this suggestion, see, among others, David Brakke, "The Body in Early Eastern Christian Sources," *Bulletin of the American Society of Papyrologists* 37 (2000): 119–134, at 123–124; King, *Secret Revelation,* 111–113.

21. Wayne A. Meeks, "The Image of the Androgyne: Some Uses of a Symbol in Earliest Christianity," *History of Religions* 13 (1974): 165–208.

22. See Anne McGuire, "Women, Gender, and Gnosis in Gnostic Texts and Traditions," in Ross Shepard Kraemer and Mary Rose D'Angelo, eds., *Women and Christian Origins* (New York: Oxford University Press, 1999), 257–299; and the essays in Karen L. King, ed., *Images of the Feminine in Gnosticism,* Studies in Antiquity and Christianity (Philadelphia: Fortress, 1988), especially Michael Williams, "Variety in Gnostic Perspectives on Gender," 2–22.

23. McGuire, "Women, Gender, and Gnosis," 268–273.

24. Irenaeus, *Against the Heresies* 1.30.11.

25. David Brakke, "The Seed of Seth at the Flood: Biblical Interpretation and Gnostic Theological Reflection," in Charles A. Bobertz and David Brakke, eds.,

*Reading in Christian Communities: Essays on Interpretation in the Early Church,* Christianity and Judaism in Antiquity 14 (Notre Dame, Ind.: University of Notre Dame Press, 2002), 41–62.

26. Bentley Layton, "Prolegomena to the Study of Ancient Gnosticism," in L. Michael White and O. Larry Yarbrough, eds., *The Social World of the First Christians: Essays in Honor of Wayne A. Meeks* (Minneapolis: Fortress, 1995), 334–350, at 336–339.

27. Heinrich von Staden, "Hairesis and Heresy: The Case of the *haireseis iatrikai,*" in B. F. Meyer and E. P. Sanders, eds., *Jewish and Christian Self-Definition,* vol. 3, *Self-Definition in the Greco-Roman World* (Philadelphia: Fortress, 1982), 76–100, at 92, 96.

28. Denise Kimber Buell, "Rethinking the Relevance of Race for Early Christian Self-Definition," *Harvard Theological Review* 94 (2001): 449–476, at 458–466.

29. Fredriksen, "Mandatory Retirement," 232.

30. Denise Kimber Buell, *Why This New Race: Ethnic Reasoning in Early Christianity* (New York: Columbia University Press, 2005). Some scholars resist the use of the term "race" in discussing ancient views of ethnicity and kinship. Buell, however, makes a good argument for not eschewing the term "race," but instead exploring the ambiguities of racialized modes of thinking in early Christian works.

31. Buell, *Why This New Race,* 120–126.

32. Epiphanius of Salamis, *Against the Heresies* 39.

33. Buell, "Rethinking the Relevance of Race," 466–472.

34. Williams, *Rethinking "Gnosticism,"* 189–212.

35. Luther H. Martin, "Genealogy and Sociology in the Apocalypse of Adam," in James E. Goehring et al., eds., *Gnosticism and the Early Christian World: In Honor of James M. Robinson,* Forum Fascicles (Sonoma, Calif.: Polebridge Press, 1990), 25–36.

36. Jean-Marie Sevrin, *Le dossier baptismal Séthien: Études sur la sacramentaire gnostique,* Bibliothèque copte de Nag Hammadi, Section "Études," 2 (Québec: Les presses de l'Université Laval, 1986), provides the most thorough study, but for an excellent short discussion, see John D. Turner, "Ritual in Gnosticism," in John D. Turner and Ruth Majercik, eds., *Gnosticism and Later Platonism: Themes, Figures, and Texts,* Society of Biblical Literature Symposium Series 12 (Atlanta: Society of Biblical Literature, 2000), 83–139, at 87–97.

37. For example, see also *Melchizedek* 7:25–9:4; 16:11–17.

38. The five steps mentioned here appear earlier in the work in a different order: glorification, enthroning, enrobing, baptism, and becoming light (45:13–20).

39. Alastair H. B. Logan, "The Mystery of the Five Seals: Gnostic Initiation Reconsidered," *Vigiliae Christianae* 51 (1997): 188–206, gives an excellent overview of the possibilities and suggests the anointing of eyes, ears, and mouth.

40. Turner, "Ritual in Gnosticism," 128–137.

41. Plato, *Symposium* 210a–212a.

42. Cicero, *Republic* 6.9–26.

43. On this work, see Karen L. King, *A Revelation of the Unknowable God: A Gnostic Text from the Nag Hammadi Library,* California Classical Library (Sonoma, Calif.: Polebridge, 1996).

44. Epiphanius of Salamis, *Against the Heresies* 40.7.2.

45. Zeke Mazur, "Self-Manifestation and 'Primary Revelation' in the Platonizing Sethian Ascent Treatises and Plotinian Mysticism" (paper delivered at the Annual Meeting of the Society of Biblical Literature, Boston, Mass., November 2008).

46. Porphyry, *Life of Plotinus* 16.

47. Mazur, "Self-Manifestation and 'Primary Revelation.' "

48. On the rise and fall of this approach, see Karen L. King, *What Is Gnosticism?* (Cambridge: Harvard University Press, 2003), 71–109.

49. For example, Birger A. Pearson, *Gnosticism and Christianity in Roman and Coptic Egypt,* Studies in Antiquity & Christianity (New York: T & T Clark, 2004).

50. The classic statement of this view is Robert M. Grant, *Gnosticism and Early Christianity* (New York: Columbia University Press, 1959), 27–38.

51. Carl B. Smith, *No Longer Jews: The Search for Gnostic Origins* (Peabody, Mass.: Hendrickson, 2004).

52. Birger A. Pearson, *Gnosticism, Judaism, and Egyptian Christianity,* Studies in Antiquity and Christianity (Minneapolis: Fortress, 1990), 51.

53. For critical discussion and examples, see Williams, *Rethinking "Gnosticism,"* 225–229.

54. Zlatko Pleše, *Poetics of the Gnostic Universe: Narrative and Cosmology in the "Apocryphon of John,"* Nag Hammadi and Manichaean Studies 52 (Leiden: Brill, 2006), 15–16.

55. Williams, *Rethinking "Gnosticism,"* 226–227.

56. Daniel Boyarin, "Justin Martyr Invents Judaism," *Church History* 70 (2001): 427–461.

57. Clement of Alexandria says that the followers of Prodicus called themselves Gnostics (*Stromateis* 3.4.30.1), but he does not tell us enough about his teachings to be certain that he belongs to the Gnostic school of thought. The teachings of Saturninus of Antioch, as reported by Irenaeus (*Against the Heresies* 1.24.1–2), resemble those of the Gnostics, but Irenaeus does not call him one.

58. Porphyry, *Life of Plotinus* 16.

59. Frederik Wisse, "Stalking Those Elusive Sethians," in Bentley Layton, ed., *The Rediscovery of Gnosticism: Proceedings of the International Conference on Gnosticism at Yale, New Haven, Connecticut, March 28–31, 1978,* vol. 2,

*Sethian Gnosticism*, Studies in the History of Religions (Leiden: Brill, 1981), 563–576.

60. Alan B. Scott, "Churches or Books? Sethian Social Organization," *Journal of Early Christian Studies* 3 (1995): 109–122.

61. Hans-Martin Schenke, "The Phenomenon and Significance of Gnostic Sethianism," in Layton, *Rediscovery of Gnosticism*, vol. 2, *Sethian Gnosticism*, 588–616.

62. John D. Turner, *Sethian Gnosticism and the Platonic Tradition*, Bibliothèque copte de Nag Hammadi, "Études," 6 (Louvain: Peeters, 2001), 255–304.

63. Compare the orders of the aeons reality, blessedness, and vitality in *Zōstrianos* 14:1–15:17 and *The Foreigner* 60:12–35.

64. King, *Secret Revelation*, vii.

## 4. Unity and Diversity in Second-Century Rome

1. The best short account of this conflict is Paula Fredriksen, "Judaism, the Circumcision of Gentiles, and Apocalyptic Hope: Another Look at Galatians 1 and 2," *Journal of Theological Studies*, n.s. 42 (1991): 532–564.

2. Peter Lampe, *From Paul to Valentinus: Christians at Rome in the First Two Centuries*, trans. Michael Steinhauser (Minneapolis: Fortress, 2003).

3. Einar Thomassen, "Orthodoxy and Heresy in Second-Century Rome," *Harvard Theological Review* 97 (2004): 241–256, at 248.

4. For a recent treatment, see Harry Y. Gamble, "Marcion and the 'Canon,'" in Margaret M. Mitchell and Frances M. Young, eds., *The Cambridge History of Christianity*, vol. 2, *Origins to Constantine* (Cambridge: Cambridge University Press, 2006), 195–213.

5. Andrew McGowan, "Marcion's Love of Creation," *Journal of Early Christian Studies* 9 (2001): 295–311, at 303–304.

6. Ibid.

7. Gerd Lüdemann, "The History of Earliest Christianity in Rome: I. Valentinus and Marcion; II. Ptolemaeus and Justin," *Journal of Higher Criticism* 2 (1995): 112–141, at 113–123; Lampe, *From Paul to Valentinus*, 392–393.

8. Irenaeus, *Against the Heresies* 1.11.1.

9. Ibid.; Anne McGuire, "Valentinus and the *Gnōstikē Hairesis*: An Investigation of Valentinus's Place in the History of Gnosticism" (Ph.D. diss., Yale University, 1983).

10. For an excellent treatment of Valentinus's thought, see David Dawson, *Allegorical Readers and Cultural Revision in Ancient Alexandria* (Berkeley: University of California Press, 1992), 127–182.

11. Bentley Layton, *The Gnostic Scriptures: A New Translation with Annotations and Introductions* (Garden City, N.Y.: Doubleday, 1987), 217.

12. Thomassen, "Orthodoxy and Heresy," 241–246.

13. *Gospel of Truth:* Beniot Standaert, "'L'évangile de vérité': Critique et lecture," *New Testament Studies* 22 (1976): 243–275. *On Free Will:* Ismo Dunderberg, *Beyond Gnosticism: Myth, Lifestyle, and Society in the School of Valentinus* (New York: Columbia University Press, 2008), 67–72.

14. Irenaeus, *Against the Heresies* 1.11.1; *Gospel of Truth* 17:4–18:11; Dawson, *Allegorical Readers and Cultural Revision,* 145–147.

15. Layton, *Gnostic Scriptures,* 248.

16. Dunderberg, *Beyond Gnosticism,* 60–67; Layton, *Gnostic Scriptures,* 222, 250–251.

17. Fragments C and D, Clement of Alexandria, *Stromateis* 2.36, 4.89–90, in Layton, *Gnostic Scriptures,* 234–237. For discussions see Dawson, *Allegorical Readers and Cultural Revision,* 136–143, and Dunderberg, *Beyond Gnosticism,* 46–59.

18. Fragment A, Hippolytus, *Refutation* 6.42.2, in Layton, *Gnostic Scriptures,* 230–231.

19. Fragment E, Clement of Alexandria, *Stromateis* 3.59.3, in Layton, *Gnostic Scriptures,* 238–239.

20. *Gospel of Truth* 18:24–34.

21. Fragment A, in Layton, *Gnostic Scriptures,* 231.

22. *Gospel of Truth* 43:1–15.

23. Fragment G, in Layton, *Gnostic Scriptures,* 243.

24. *Gospel of Truth* 23:8–10.

25. Clement of Alexandria, *Stromateis* 7.17.

26. Hans von Campenhausen, *Ecclesiastical Authority and Spiritual Power in the Church of the First Three Centuries* (London: Black, 1969), 157–160, 201; Elaine H. Pagels, "Visions, Appearances, and Apostolic Authority: Gnostic and Orthodox Traditions," in Barbara Aland, ed., *Gnosis: Festschrift für Hans Jonas* (Göttingen: Vandenhoeck & Ruprecht, 1978), 415–430, at 426.

27. Bentley Layton, "The Significance of Basilides in Ancient Christian Thought," *Representations* 28 (1989): 135–151, at 135–36.

28. Einar Thomassen, *The Spiritual Seed: The Church of the "Valentinians,"* Nag Hammadi and Manichaean Studies 60 (Leiden: Brill, 2006), 492; Dunderberg, *Beyond Gnosticism,* 63.

29. *Gospel of Truth* 33:5–15.

30. Ibid., 19:34–23:17.

31. Ibid., 25:7–25.

32. Thomassen, "Orthodoxy and Heresy," 253–254.

33. Justin, *Dialogue with Trypho* 1–8.

34. Harlow Gregory Snyder, "'Above the Bath of Myrtinus': Justin Martyr's 'School' in the City of Rome," *Harvard Theological Review* 100 (2007): 335–362, at 349.

35. Josephus, *Life* 10; Clement of Alexandria, *Stromateis* 7.15.92.3; Heinrich von Staden, "Hairesis and Heresy: The Case of the *haireseis iatrikai*," in B. F. Meyer and E. P. Sanders, eds., *Jewish and Christian Self-Definition*, vol. 3, *Self-Definition in the Greco-Roman World* (Philadelphia: Fortress, 1982), 76–100, at 96–97.

36. Justin, *Dialogue with Trypho* 35.3.

37. *Against All the Schools of Thought:* Justin, *First Apology* 26; *Against Marcion:* Irenaeus, *Against the Heresies* 4.6.

38. Justin, *Dialogue with Trypho* 35.4–6.

39. Ibid., 80.3–5.

40. Alain Le Boulluec, *Le Notion d'hérésie dans la literature grecque IIᵉ-IIIᵉ siècles* (Paris: Études augustiniennes, 1985), 37.

41. Justin, *First Apology* 26; *Dialogue with Trypho* 35.2.

42. Valentinus, Fragment G, in Layton, *Gnostic Scriptures,* 243.

43. Justin, *Second Apology* 10, 13.

44. For this perspective on Justin, see Rebecca Lyman, "Hellenism and Heresy," *Journal of Early Christian Studies* 11 (2003): 209–222, esp. 218–219.

45. On this point and this entire paragraph, see Lyman, "Hellenism and Heresy," 219. Quotation: Justin, *Dialogue with Trypho* 35.5.

46. Justin, *First Apology* 5.

47. Justin, *Dialogue with Trypho* 35, 80.

48. Ibid., 55.1; 56.1.

49. See especially Justin, *First Apology* 64.5; *Second Apology* 5(6).3. I am not persuaded by the arguments of Denis Minns and Paul Parvis against this interpretation (*Justin, Philosopher and Martyr: Apologies,* Oxford Early Christian Texts [Oxford: Oxford University Press, 2009], 62–65).

## 5. Strategies of Self-Differentiation

1. There are several editions of the Abercius inscription. I have consulted Rosalinde A. Kearsley, "The Epitaph of Aberkios: The Earliest Christian Inscription?" *New Documents Illustrating Early Christianity* 6 (1997):177–181.

2. Eusebius, *History of the Church* 5.16.

3. On Abercius, his inscription, and the anti-Montanist treatise addressed to him, see William Tabbernee, *Prophets and Gravestones: An Imaginative History of Montanists and Other Early Christians* (Peabody, Mass.: Hendrickson, 2009), 43–46.

4. Eusebius, *History of the Church* 5.16.

5. George W. MacRae, "Why the Church Rejected Gnosticism," in his *Studies in the New Testament and Gnosticism,* Good News Studies 26 (Wilmington, Del.: Michael Glazier, 1987), 251–262.

6. Karlfried Froehlich, "Montanism and Gnosis," in David Neiman and Margaret Schatkin, eds., *The Heritage of the Early Church: Essays in Honor of*

*the Very Reverend Georges Vasilievich Florovsky on the Occasion of his Eightieth Birthday* (Rome: Pontificia Institutum Studiorum Orientalium, 1973), 91–111.

7. For this perspective on Valentinianism, see especially Ismo Dunderberg, *Beyond Gnosticism: Myth, Lifestyle, and Society in the School of Valentinus* (New York: Columbia University Press, 2008).

8. Irenaeus, *Against the Heresies* 1.7.1.

9. *Tripartite Tractate* 132:16–23 (trans. Einar Thomassen in Marvin Meyer, ed., *The Nag Hammadi Scriptures: The International Edition* [New York: HarperOne, 2007], 99).

10. Clement of Alexandria, *Excerpts from Theodotus* 63.

11. See Dunderberg, *Beyond Gnosticism*, 77–94.

12. Irenaeus, *Against the Heresies* 1.pref.1.

13. Dunderberg, *Beyond Gnosticism*, 134–158.

14. Irenaeus, *Against the Heresies* 1.pref.2.

15. Ibid., 5.31.2.

16. *Treatise on Resurrection* 49:13–16.

17. Ptolemy, *Letter to Flora*, in Epiphanius, *Against Heresies* 33.3.1; *Treatise on Resurrection* 44:9–10.

18. Origen, *Commentary on John* 6.92.

19. Ibid., 13.95–97.

20. Elaine H. Pagels, *The Gnostic Paul: Gnostic Exegesis of the Pauline Letters* (Philadelphia: Trinity Press International, 1975).

21. Clement of Alexandria, *Stromateis* 7.17.

22. Ptolemy, *Letter to Flora*, in Epiphanius, *Against the Heresies* 33.7.9–10.

23. *Gospel According to Philip* 74:16–18.

24. *Prayer of Paul the Apostle*.

25. Einar Thomassen, *The Spiritual Seed: The Church of the "Valentinians,"* Nag Hammadi and Manichaean Studies 60 (Leiden: Brill, 2006), 333–394.

26. Clement of Alexandria, *Excerpts from Theodotus* 78.2.

27. Nicole Denzey Lewis, "*Apolytrosis* as Ritual and Sacrament: Determing a Ritual Context for Death in Marcosian Valentinianism," *Journal of Early Christian Studies* 17 (2009): 525–561.

28. Baptism: Thomassen, *Spiritual Seed*, 97–100. Separate ritual: John D. Turner, "Ritual in Gnosticism," in John D. Turner and Ruth Majercik, eds., *Gnosticism and Later Platonism: Themes, Figures, and Texts*, Society of Biblical Literature Symposium Series 12 (Atlanta: Society of Biblical Literature, 2000), 83–139, at 111–118.

29. Ambrose of Milan, *Letters* 40.16; 41.1.

30. Irenaeus, *Against the Heresies* 1.pref.2. Henceforth I will refer to this work as *AH* parenthetically in the text.

31. Virginia Burrus, "Hierarchalization and Genderization of Leadership in the Writings of Irenaeus," *Studia Patristica* 21 (1989): 42–48, at 44.

32. James L. Kugel and Rowan A. Greer, *Early Biblical Interpretation*, Library of Early Christianity (Philadelphia: Westminster, 1986), 155–176.

33. See Peter Lampe, *From Paul to Valentinus: Christians at Rome in the First Two Centuries*, trans. Michael Steinhauser (Minneapolis: Fortress, 2003), 385–396.

34. On a similar situation in early third-century Carthage, see William Tabbernee, "To Pardon or Not to Pardon? North African Montanism and the Forgiveness of Sins," *Studia Patristica* 36 (2001): 375–386.

35. Eusebius, *History of the Church* 5.20.

36. Irenaeus, *Syriac Fragment* 28; Eusebius, *History of the Church* 5.15.

37. Victor and New Prophecy: Tertullian, *Against Praxeas* 1. Victor and Theodotus: Eusebius, *History of the Church* 5.28.

38. Eusebius, *History of the Church* 5.24.

39. Irenaeus, *Proof of the Apostolic Preaching* 5–6.

40. Ibid., 47.

41. Ibid., 9.

42. "Domesticated *gnōsis*": David Dawson, *Allegorical Readers and Cultural Revision in Ancient Alexandria* (Berkeley: University of California Press, 1992), 222.

43. Clement of Alexandria, *Stromateis* 1.9.43–45. Henceforth I will refer to this work as *Str.* parenthetically in the text.

44. Eusebius, *History of the Church* 6.6; Gustave Bardy, "Aux origines de l'école d'Alexandrie," *Recherches de science religieuse* 27 (1937): 65–90; Dawson, *Allegorical Readers*, 219–222.

45. Denise Kimber Buell, *Making Christians: Clement of Alexandria and the Rhetoric of Legitimacy* (Princeton: Princeton University Press, 1999).

46. Buell, *Making Christians*, 66–68, whose translation I have adapted.

47. Ibid., 84–86.

48. On Clement's and Origen's semi-bounded canons, see R. P. C. Hanson, *Origen's Doctrine of Tradition* (London: S. P. C. K., 1954), 127–173.

49. The evidence for Clement himself having been a presbyter is weak: see Hugo Koch, "War Klemens von Alexandrien Priester?", *Zeitschrift für die neutestamentliche Wissenschaft und die Kunde der älteren Kirche* 20 (1921): 43–48.

50. Clement of Alexandria, *Who Is the Rich Man Who Is Being Saved?* 41–42.

51. Clement of Alexandria, *The Tutor* 1.21.1–2; 42.1–2.

52. Eusebius, *History of the Church* 6.2.

53. Origen, *On First Principles* pref.10. Henceforth I will refer to this work as *FP* parenthetically in the text.

54. See especially Books 2 and 3 of *On First Principles*.

55. Origen, *Commentary on John* 6.199.

56. Ibid., 2.100; 2.137–138; 6.109; 13.57–74; 13.98; 13.107–108. Cross-referencing: Frances M. Young, *Biblical Exegesis and the Formation of Christian Culture* (Cambridge: Cambridge University Press, 1997), 130–139.

57. Origen, *Commentary on John* 13.98.

58. Ibid., 6.116.

59. On these events, see Joseph Wilson Trigg, *Origen: The Bible and Philosophy in the Third-Century Church* (Atlanta: John Knox, 1983), 130–140; and Stephen J. Davis, *The Early Coptic Papacy: The Egyptian Church and Its Leadership in Late Antiquity* (Cairo: American University in Cairo Press, 2004), 22–28.

60. Trigg, *Origen*, 174–176.

61. Origen, *Homily on Numbers* 2.1; *Commentary on John* 1.10.

62. Joseph Wilson Trigg, "The Charismatic Intellectual: Origen's Understanding of Religious Leadership," *Church History* 50 (1981): 5–19; Hanson, *Origen's Doctrine of Tradition*, 73-90.

63. Eusebius, *History of the Church* 5.16.

64. Turner and Majercik, *Gnosticism and Later Platonism*; John D. Turner, *Sethian Gnosticism and the Platonic Tradition*, Bibliothèque copte de Nag Hammadi, "Études," 6 (Louvain: Peeters, 2001).

65. See the works of Cyprian of Carthage, especially *The Unity of the Church* and *The Lapsed*, along with J. Patout Burns, Jr., *Cyprian the Bishop*, Routledge Early Christian Monographs (London: Routledge, 2002).

66. Eusebius, *History of the Church* 6.33.

67. Ibid., 7.30.18–19.

68. Eusebius, *Life of Constantine* 2.68.

69. Eusebius, *History of the Church* 10.6–7

70. Eusebius, *Life of Constantine* 3.4–14.

71. *Theodosian Code* 16.5.21.

72. Michael Allen Williams, *Rethinking "Gnosticism": An Argument for Dismantling a Dubious Category* (Princeton: Princeton University Press, 1996), 292.

# SELECTED BIBLIOGRAPHY OF
# PRIMARY SOURCES IN TRANSLATION

Clement of Alexandria. *Stromateis* and Other Works. In *Fathers of the Second Century: Hermas, Tatian, Athenagoras, Theophilus, and Clement of Alexandria (Entire)*, 163–605. Vol. 2 of *The Ante-Nicene Fathers: Translations of the Writings of the Fathers Down to A.D. 325*. Ed. Alexander Roberts, James Donaldson, and A. Cleveland Coxe. Repr. Grand Rapids, Mich.: Eerdmans, 1989.

Eusebius. *The History of the Church from Christ to Constantine*. Trans. G. A. Williamson. Rev. and ed. Andrew Louth. London: Penguin, 1989.

Hippolytus. *The Refutation of All Heresies*. In *Fathers of the Third Century: Hippolytus, Cyprian, Caius, Novatian*, 9–162. Vol. 3 of *The Ante-Nicene Fathers: Translations of the Writings of the Fathers Down to A.D. 325*. Ed. Alexander Roberts, James Donaldson, and A. Cleveland Coxe. Repr. Grand Rapids, Mich.: Eerdmans, 1989.

Irenaeus of Lyons. *Against the Heresies (Detection and Overthrow of Gnōsis Falsely So-Called)*. In Robert M. Grant. *Irenaeus of Lyons*. The Early Church Fathers. London: Routledge, 1997.

———. *Proof of the Apostolic Preaching*. Trans. Joseph P. Smith, S.J. Ancient Christian Writers 16. New York: Paulist, 1952.

Justin Martyr. *Dialogue with Trypho*. Trans. Thomas B. Falls and Thomas P. Halton. Ed. Michael Slusser. Selections from the Fathers of the Church 3. Washington: Catholic University of America Press, 2003.

———. *First and Second Apologies*. In *Justin, Philosopher and Martyr: Apologies*. Ed. and trans. Denis Minns and Paul Parvis. Oxford Early Christian Texts. Oxford: Oxford University Press, 2009.

Layton, Bentley, ed. *The Gnostic Scriptures: A New Translation with Annotations and Introductions*. Garden City, N.Y.: Doubleday, 1987.

Meyer, Marvin, ed. *The Nag Hammadi Scriptures: The International Edition*. New York: HarperOne, 2007.

Origen. *Commentary on the Gospel According to John Books 1–10*. Trans. Ronald E. Heine. The Fathers of the Church 80. Washington: Catholic University of America Press, 1989.

———. *Commentary on John* [Book 1 and Book 13.3–192]. In *Origen*, 103–178. Joseph. W. Trigg. The Early Church Fathers. London: Routledge, 1998.

———. *On First Principles*. Trans. G. W. Butterworth. Gloucester, Mass.: Peter Smith, 1973.

# INDEX

Harvard University Press is a member of Green Press Initiative (greenpressinitiative.org), a nonprofit organization working to help publishers and printers increase their use of recycled paper and decrease their use of fiber derived from endangered forests. This book was printed on recycled paper containing 30% post-consumer waste and processed chlorine free.